'The book is written as simple, straightforward advice in which complicated material is made easy to understand. The language is reader-friendly and accommodates our differences with great understanding.'

— *Tidsskrift for Psykoterapi*
(Journal of Psychotherapy)

'Ilse Sand guides you with simple advice and concrete exercises through the labyrinth of emotions, so you can learn to let go of old, unwelcome patterns and start working through your emotions – and, more to the point, achieve a greater acceptance and understanding of your feelings and the feelings of others.'

— *Magasinet Psykologi*
(Psychology Magazine)

by the same author

Highly Sensitive People in an Insensitive World
How to Create a Happy Life
Ilse Sand
Translated by Elisabeth Svanholmer
ISBN 978 1 78592 066 0
eISBN 978 1 78450 324 6

THE EMOTIONAL COMPASS

HOW TO THINK BETTER ABOUT YOUR FEELINGS

ILSE SAND

Jessica Kingsley *Publishers*
London and Philadelphia

First published by Forlaget Ammentorp, Denmark in 2011

English language edition first published in 2017
by Jessica Kingsley Publishers
73 Collier Street
London N1 9BE, UK
and
400 Market Street, Suite 400
Philadelphia, PA 19106, USA

www.jkp.com

Copyright © Ilse Sand 2011, 2017
English language edition translated by Nina Sokol

Library of Congress Cataloging in Publication Data
Names: Sand, Ilse, author.
Title: The emotional compass : how to think better about your feelings / Ilse Sand.
Other titles: Find nye veje i f?lelsernes labyrint. English
Description: London ; Philadelphia : Jessica Kingsley Publishers, [2017] |
    "First published by Forlaget Ammentorp, Denmark in 2011." | Includes index.
Identifiers: LCCN 2016015815 | ISBN 9781785921278 (alk. paper)
Subjects: LCSH: Emotions. | Self-perception.
Classification: LCC BF561 .S26413 2017 | DDC 152.4--dc23 LC record
available at https://urldefense.proofpoint.com/v2/url?u=https-3A__
lccn.loc.gov_2016015815&d=BQIFAg&c=euGZstcaTDllvimEN8b7jXrwqOf-
v5A_CdpgnVfiiMM&r=jDhEGalRBceh95Jy341lNgmWR9tnCifzbrA2NWHfa
H8&m=0CCE5Br0LYMRXf9xAf7oQ5R9KjZTcVuKq0oTBLxQyOE&s=_
qnp6sNQy_9pRH5BjpuOa20svQBIhermhKkw8LOseXA&e=

British Library Cataloguing in Publication Data
A CIP catalogue record for this book is available from the British Library

ISBN 978 1 78592 127 8
eISBN 978 1 78450 392 5

Printed and bound in the United States

CONTENTS

PREFACE

This book is written for those who would like to become more knowledgeable about themselves on an emotional level. It is also written for psychotherapists, psychologists and other practitioners who help people with their emotional problems.

Through the many years that I have conducted courses and lectured on psychology I have discovered the significant role that case studies play when you are trying to make complicated material more accessible to a wider audience. So in this book I have used numerous examples deriving from the lives of my clients and course participants, not to mention my own life.

The knowledge that I convey in this book is knowledge that I have previously expressed through the years, partly in my work as a course organiser and lecturer and partly in my work as a therapist. I have seen how an improved knowledge of the way in which psychological mechanisms work and are connected has made life easier for the people I have been in contact with. I am now hoping to reach a wider audience with this book.

My straightforward approach when giving advice in this book is not meant to be seen as an instruction on how to live life in the only 'correct' way. People are very different and there is never a right way to do things that applies to everyone. Find your own way, see my advice as mere suggestions which you can choose either to follow or not, and sense whether it feels right for you. Your path may be an entirely different one which I have not yet encountered.

You will get more out of the book if you read it from start to finish, but it is also possible to read each chapter independently of the rest of the book, just as you use a reference book.

Ilse Sand

Introduction

For many years I have listened to people tell their stories, both as a vicar and later as a psychotherapist. I have also often followed their joys and hardships in life at close range over a longer period of time.

It has often struck me how many of the problems derive from a lack of general knowledge about feelings. Some people are stuck in unhealthy patterns because they are trying to change something that can't be altered. Others weep over circumstances that could, in fact, be altered; while still others find themselves caught in unnecessary conflicts owing to inappropriate thought habits which could be rectified if they had the necessary knowledge to do so.

I have seen how people are able to find their way once they have gained the necessary knowledge. How, in their increased knowledge of the way the psychology of emotions works, they are able to find the extra energy they need to alter the things in their life that can be changed and to let go of wanting to control the things they have no control over.

My intention with this book is to convey psychological connections in a language that is easily understandable and which refers back to real experiences. Once you know what you actually feel, and why, finding your way in life will become much easier.

Chapter 1

Finding Your Primary Feeling in the Present

Emotions are not always what they seem to be. For example, if you see a woman who is crying you will probably think she is sad. But she may also be scared or angry. The fact is that it is typical for women to conceal several different feelings while wearing a hat of 'sadness'.

If you see a man who expresses anger you cannot be entirely sure that that is what he is in fact feeling, because it is typical for men also to express anger when they are in reality scared, sad, depressed or experiencing a crisis. Sometimes we are not even sure ourselves what it is we are primarily feeling. The more you become aware of your exact feelings, the easier it is to take action.

You can distinguish between basic feelings and mixed feelings. A basic feeling may be universally registered by all people and the more advanced species of animals. All other feelings may be described as being a variation of mixtures of the basic feelings.

There is some disagreement as to which feelings ought to be considered basic feelings. But therapists agree that the following four feelings belong to this category:

~ Happiness

~ Sadness

~ Fear/anxiety

~ Anger.

And these four are adequate when explaining most of the emotions we feel. For example, disappointment is a blend of sadness and anger; while feeling tense may be a blend of anxiety and happiness.

If I am unsure what it is I am feeling, I will ask myself the following questions based on those four feelings:

'Is there something that I am angry about?'

'Is there something I am sad about?'

'Could I be scared of something?'

'Is there possibly a sense of happiness that is hardly being acknowledged or registered?'

Once I have the answers to these questions it becomes much easier for me to put what I am feeling into words.

The various degrees of feelings: being aware of the first tentative beginnings

Often we won't register a feeling until it has gained a certain degree of strength. If 0 represents no feeling, and 10 represents the strongest level of feeling that you know, you may not discover the feeling until you have reached, for example, 5. If you take the feeling of *happiness*, for example, the first tentative beginnings give you a light sensation of something feeling pleasant. If it gains full strength, you will probably feel like singing, dancing or embracing someone.

You can practise becoming aware of even the first tentative beginnings of the feeling. You will get more pleasure out of it if you learn how to discover it even if it is only fleeting and only reaches a 2 in strength. Perhaps you became happy because a ray of sun brushed your cheek or a passer-by smiled at you.

Wanting to embrace
someone, kiss and dance

Feeling a sense of warmth

Feeling a sense of inner joy

Feeling enthusiastic

Feeling light

Sensing energy

Having the feeling that there
are bubbles in your stomach

Light sensation of
something pleasant

The feeling of happiness

Also the feeling of *sadness* can be felt in various degrees. If you discover your feeling of sadness at a relatively early point you will have more energy to decide how you want to relate to it. In Chapter 6 you can read about how you can choose to either distance yourself from the feeling or give into it completely, and thereby 'mourn' your way through it.

Wanting to die

Longing for eternal sleep

Great fatigue

Deeply unhappy

Sobbing

Wanting to cry

Trembling face

A lump in your throat

Tears in your eyes

Heaviness in your body

A feeling of 'ugh'

Somewhat fatigued

The feeling of sadness

When it comes to *anger* it is particularly important to discover it as soon as possible. Once you have reached the point of losing your temper it is difficult to think clearly because at that point we tend to think in dichotomies like black/white, and our capacity to empathise with the other party decreases.

When I teach about anger I sometimes ask the participants to examine how they sense the tentative beginnings of their anger. Some report having a sensation of cold, others of warmth. Yet others get a distinctive feeling in their stomach when something starts to irritate them. If you practise sensing your body it can help you to discover the feelings, even if they are only slightly present.

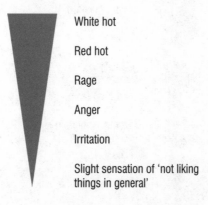

White hot

Red hot

Rage

Anger

Irritation

Slight sensation of 'not liking things in general'

The feeling of anger

The strength of your feelings will vary depending on the relationship you are dealing with. If your feelings are connected with another person's then, typically, the more they mean to you the stronger your feelings will be, including the negative ones. The fact is that if the one you love does not give you what you feel you need in return it will particularly hurt. It won't hurt nearly as much if the person in question is the local shop owner or the postman.

If you have been brought up to be as accommodating as possible and not burden other people with your feelings, it will be extremely difficult to be in close relationships. I think that sometimes this may be the unconscious reason why some people remain single and simply never meet the right person. Because if they were to meet someone who declared their love to them, they would become afraid of their own feelings and so, in order to protect themselves, they would quickly find some flaws with the other person and use these as an excuse to pull back. 'He wasn't the right one for me,' is what they will say to themselves and to others.

Discover your feeling by way of your thoughts

Sometimes when I am sitting with a client who tells me that she is sad, I can sense that there may be other feelings at play. In such a case, the client's thoughts can be good signposts. Thoughts and feelings are closely connected. That is why I always ask, 'What thought is connected with the feeling you are having right now?' If the thought is, 'It wasn't right of him to treat me that way,' the feeling is probably not one of sadness but of anger. If your thought is a moral judgment of others, the feeling is anger. That also applies if your thoughts revolve around unfair treatment.

Typical thoughts during happiness

~ How lucky I am.

~ How beautiful that is.

~ What a wonderful day.

~ Tomorrow it will be even better.

~ It could have been much worse. I'm glad it wasn't.

Typical thoughts during sadness

Thoughts about something you would have liked to have had. Perhaps you were thinking about how wonderful it would have been to have taken that trip that had to be cancelled because of an unexpected bill. Or in your mind you see the person you would really like to have brought with you but who chose to prioritise something else.

Or your thoughts may revolve around the fact that you would have liked to have been slimmer, more beautiful, more intelligent or more charming.

Typical thoughts during fear/anxiety

~ It won't work.

~ I can't stand this.

~ I can't handle this.

~ I won't be able to make it on time.

~ This is dangerous.

Typical thoughts during anger

~ He should have been more considerate of me (moral judgment).

~ I should have discovered it sooner (moral judgment directed at yourself – introverted anger).

~ It is unfair.

~ I'm being cheated.

. . . .

If you are not sure which feeling you are having you can try directing your attention to your thoughts to find the answer. Another possibility is to discover your feeling by examining what it is you want.

Finding your feeling through what you want

Within a feeling there is an impulse, a desire for movement. For example, take the word 'emotion'. Emotion means a movement of the feelings. You can find the feeling by listening to the movement. Use your imagination and create an inner image of an act that you or someone else is doing which would make your body feel satisfied at this very moment.

Some people get a sense of restlessness or discontent in their body, but don't know for sure what it is or why. If the sense of restlessness is, for example, felt in your legs, I will typically ask what the legs feel like doing. If they feel like running away the feeling is probably anxiety. If they feel like kicking it is probably anger.

If you are angry you probably feel like doing an aggressive act. However, it may be so forbidden that you can't feel it yourself. Perhaps you cannot even feel your own anger and are in doubt as to whether it is even there. Try imagining that the person you are angry with is standing before you and that he or she slips on a banana peel, and try sensing what that does to you. If your face lights up and you are laughing you might be angry.

If you are unsure of what feeling it is that you are sensing at a given moment, the new path for you may be to ask yourself, 'What does my body feel like doing right now?' By focusing on what your body wants, you can discover what feeling is at play.

Admit to your feelings, but do not be blindly led by them

You are not your feelings. Feelings cannot be identified as something we are but, rather, as something we have.

Try distancing yourself from the particular feeling you are experiencing and decide whether you want to give in to it or whether you want to go against it. Be aware of the fact that you do have a choice.

While writing this book, I take breaks every now and then, print out some chapters and sit down to read them. At times I think that what I have written is a useless and incoherent mess. I become sad and want to throw it all into the bin. But this is when I decide to go against my feeling and my desire. I force myself to sit with it a little longer and often what will happen is that I will suddenly discover a new way of structuring it so that it makes better sense.

Perhaps you, too, have noticed that by remaining in the chaos instead of fleeing from it you often discover that something entirely new emerges as a result.

Summary

Feelings are something we have, not something we are. We can choose to either give in to the feeling we are experiencing in the present or distance ourselves from it and do something else. The more exactly you can identify what it is you are feeling at this very moment, the easier it is to find your way.

If you are unsure what you are feeling, you can examine the thoughts that are connected with the feeling or ask yourself what your body feels like doing right now.

Chapter 2

Distance Yourself from Your Thoughts

Thoughts and feelings are closely linked. They affect one another in a reciprocal interplay.

You cannot govern your feelings directly. For example, if you receive a Christmas present that you think is ugly you cannot suddenly decide that you like it. At the most, you can pretend that you do. Similarly, you cannot deny your feelings of anger or jealousy even though it would be so much more practical to be without those feelings.

However, you are not at the complete mercy of those feelings because you can affect them by way of your thoughts. Though you cannot be in charge of your feelings, you can influence your thoughts and you can choose what you want to focus on.

The same event can awaken many feelings, all depending on how you think about them. Let us say, for example, that you receive a gift from your neighbour. If your first thought is, 'What is his agenda?' you might get scared. If you start thinking, 'Who does he think he is? We haven't made any agreements about exchanging gifts, and now I'll have to find a way to repay him,' you will feel anger. If you think, 'He must be having a great day since he feels like giving his neighbour a present,' the feeling will be neutral. And if you think to yourself, 'He probably thinks I'm a wonderful person,' you will be happy.

Think realistically

There is a lot of focus on positive thinking these days. Some people are so good at it that they end up having a filter between themselves and reality. No matter what they experience they turn it into something positive. When other people bother them they think that the intention is probably good. And they may never discover how little they are actually getting out of their relationships and therefore choose to remain in something they really ought to consider getting out of.

It is not just a matter of thinking as positively as possible. If you are too naïve, things may go very wrong for you. If I think to myself that I am a person who everyone likes, I will be in for a huge shock and may even experience a crisis the day I discover that it is quite clear that there are people out there who aren't necessarily pleased with me.

So that is why you should try to think as realistically as possible. If you see the world around you as too positive, you need to clean your eyeglasses so that you are better able to see the world as it really is. That way you will be much better at navigating in it.

If you have a tendency to think negatively, you will also need to clean your eyeglasses so that you are better able to see the world and yourself independently of negative distortions. If you can manage to do that, your mood and level of energy will rise. It is important that you think as realistically as possible: not too negatively and not too positively.

Always remember, you are not your thoughts. Thoughts are things you have. And it is important to keep them at a suitable distance.

Look at your thoughts objectively, as if they belong to someone else. It is a very good idea to write them down on a piece of paper. That way, it will be easier for you to distance yourself from them. Evaluate whether they are realistic. And if you are in doubt, I highly recommend talking with others who are better able to see them objectively for the simple reason that they are not you.

Keep an eye on who you compare yourself with

Every now and then I talk with a young, unhappy person who is reading about his friends' many successful experiences on Facebook. My impression is that all the focus is on the success stories while the stories of failure tend to be silenced. In that way you can get a pretty skewed picture of what other people's lives are like.

You can always find someone to compare yourself with, someone who leaves you with a feeling of being a failure. No matter how well things are going for you, there will always be someone with whom things are going better. Some people even seem to have an almost masochistic tendency to solely compare themselves with the success stories they hear, which they tend to idealise, and this makes them thereby devalue their own successes in life.

If you have a tendency to do that, I recommend the following brief exercise. Imagine you see a person before you of the same gender who is handicapped and lives in an old people's home. Compare yourself with that person and you will experience your mood improving as you become thankful for the things you have and are able to do.

A good deal of this has to do with the kind of questions you ask yourself. If you ask, 'What could be wrong with me, since I don't have nearly as much success as the very accomplished person talked about in all the newspapers?' you are focusing on your own flaws. However, if you ask, 'How come I haven't ended up as a homeless person out on the street?' you are focusing on your resources. And if you ask, 'What are all the good things in my life?' you are focusing on the things that give you joy and hope and that you value in life.

Summary

If you tend to easily fill your mind with negative thoughts about yourself and your future or other people, a new path for you would be to focus on your thoughts. Distance yourself from them so that you can evaluate them objectively and stop them if they are not realistic or darken your mood. Then ask yourself, 'Could I have thought about this differently? Could I have focused on something else?'

Be aware of the fact that not all thoughts can be changed to something positive without there being a change in your perception of reality. And it is better to think a negative thought if it is more realistic than to think something positive if it means compromising with reality. For example, it is better to think, 'It might rain on the day I want to hold a garden party,' and make a plan B for what you might do should that be the case rather than thinking, 'Of course it won't rain that day; why should it?'

Chapter 3

Avoid Unnecessary Conflict

Take a closer look at your angry thoughts

There are certain conflicts which you cannot avoid because the price you pay for doing so is too high. If you do not draw the line and take on those conflicts, you will find that your personal space is restricted. However, there are conflicts which are unnecessary because a mere change in attitude may be enough to resolve the problem, making an open confrontation seem superfluous.

Whenever I feel myself getting angry, the first thing I do is to examine the thoughts that are connected with my anger. Perhaps my anger is due to a misinterpretation of reality on my part and will therefore disappear as soon as I rectify the mistake.

One time I was waiting for an important email on a Friday afternoon when my internet connection crashed. Time passed by and my irritation rose. As time continued to pass I began imagining how the support team for the internet had probably stopped working for the week and were celebrating the start of the weekend; how they were probably out having a good time while I sat in deep frustration waiting for them to respond. In my mind's eye I saw a group of young people who were out partying and I simply could not calm down.

Once I realised what my thoughts were doing, I altered the image. I thought about my son when he was a teenager and how troubling it had been for him whenever something was not working with his computer. I then envisioned a couple of young men working on getting the internet fixed. I saw how they were sweating with stress to get it done on time. My anger immediately declined to a level I could deal with. I was now able to concentrate on doing something else until my internet started working again, which it did an hour later.

Taking things personally

Most of us make the mistake from time to time of personifying something. In short, this basically means that you tend to think that other people do things in order to work against you or bother you somehow. It is a somewhat childish form of self-centredness. During such a moment we perceive ourselves as being the centre of the universe, just like children do, thereby forgetting that other people are most likely doing things because of their own inner state. So we are not the ones who are the centre of their universe; quite the contrary, they are.

Let's say, for example, that my son and I are supposed to meet but he comes late and I start thinking to myself, 'My son is late because he doesn't respect me. He doesn't care about my time.' But my son may have been so passionately absorbed in a project that he had forgotten all about the time, which is a tendency I myself have and which he has inherited from me. When I start thinking that way instead, I become happy instead of angry.

If I am unsure as to whether the thoughts I have that are connected with anger are right or not, I will sometimes ask the person whom I am angry with (if I am comfortable enough with the person). In this case I will tell the person what my thoughts are and will not express my anger until I have checked whether my thoughts are indeed correct.

An example of this might be a situation in which I said, 'Whenever I come to visit you and your whole house is such a mess that I can barely find a place to sit, and you know how much neatness means to me, I think to myself that you are not particularly concerned with my needs.' The person might respond by saying something like, 'I know you love for things to be tidy and neat, but I also know that you really need my presence and attention. So when I came home from an exceptionally stressful day at work I chose to go for a jog so that you wouldn't have to be burdened with my many thoughts. I am now relaxed and really ready to hear how you are doing.'

Needless to say, in such a situation my anger would immediately disappear and I would be relieved that I had avoided a fight and a possibly unpleasant atmosphere.

Anger may be due to unrealistic expectations

I was once very angry with my insurance company and was restlessly pacing back and forth across the floor as I considered how I was going to complain to them. Internally, I was in turmoil. The one thought that I kept having, and that really agitated me, was the following:

'I have been paying into that insurance company for all these years and when I finally need them they reimburse me with a ridiculously small sum.' Upon which my next thought was, 'I have been cheated.'

Sometimes your thoughts run in circles inside of you, thereby initiating various emotions. Perhaps you have noticed that you have a tendency to perceive your own thoughts as though they are reality. And if you then allow yourself to be blindly governed by the particular feelings that your thoughts awaken within you, you may end up using a lot of energy on anger and conflicts.

It can really pay off to examine your thoughts thoroughly before acting on the emotions that result from them. Distancing ourselves from our thoughts is something we do not typically want to do. It is much easier to give in to whatever thoughts and feelings arise and just go along with them. Distancing yourself from that means having to pull yourself together on some level, taking a step back and observing what it is you are doing, like you would had you been looking at the situation from the outside.

Fortunately, that was what I did before I got a chance to complain. For a while I started thinking about how insurance companies actually work and the particular disagreement I was having with them now. And it was then that I realised that my anger was based on false expectations because I was not sufficiently aware of what the reality of the situation was.

Upon reflection I could see that an insurance company does not function like a bank where as a customer you expect to withdraw the same amount that you deposited, and preferably with interest. The insurance company spends a lot of money on administration and salaries for estimators and other staff. So the amount that you pay to an insurance company should not be seen as an investment that you can expect to get a profit from. What you are really paying for is a sense of security. Once I started thinking about it in that light, my anger fell to a level where I was able to handle it and was thus able to fully concentrate on my work again.

If you spend a lot of energy being angry, it may be because your impression of reality needs to be adjusted. For example, if you see yourself as someone who deserves to get special treatment you are bound to experience a number of disappointments in life. The same is true if you think that happiness and joy are things that you have the right to demand.

This is what cartoonist Nikoline Werdelin said in an interview:

> Seeing happiness as something that lasts for long intervals at a time is one of the most destructive concepts that we have had to grow up with. Just like the word 'perfect', happiness is a concept that is not really doable since it only emerges in brief glimpses. Instead, someone should have said right after we were born, 'Hello and welcome, I just want you to know that the place where you have now arrived will sometimes really scare you, you will see yourself as being a coward, you will feel that you have betrayed someone or something, at times you will be happy and experience a little intimacy – if you are lucky, a lot – and if you learn how to read you will never be entirely alone.'

But we grow up having a different impression and that is why a feeling of great disappointment and the realisation that happiness is not long-lasting is bound to emerge at some point. Shocked, you soon discover all the anxiety and rage and misunderstandings that day-to-day life really consists of. (Cited in Knudsen 1998)

I chose to include this citation because I think it provides an interesting contrast to the focus we have nowadays on 'the happy human being'. We are bombarded with pictures of happy families by way of commercials and may therefore easily blame ourselves or, for example, our partner if our lives do not live up to the idea of how a happy person ought to be.

Many of the problems which couples experience tend to arise because one or both parties are not nearly as happy as they had expected to be, and it is much too easy to put the blame on their partner.

Summary

When you decide to distance yourself from your thoughts, and to examine the thoughts that initiate your anger more closely, you are taking greater responsibility for your emotions. It thereby becomes harder to put the blame on others by saying things like, 'Now you've made me angry.' Instead you would say, 'I got angry because I thought…'

If you are in the habit of confronting others with your anger, a new approach for you might be to examine your thoughts more thoroughly first. You will most likely notice that by doing so you will not be involved in the same amount of conflict. Moreover, you will be able to release and apply that energy more constructively.

Even though you may already be good at nipping unnecessary negative thought patterns in the bud, and in that way manage to avoid unnecessary conflicts and arguments, in the next chapter you will discover that you can encounter the kind of anger that won't allow itself to be altered through changed thought patterns or attitudes or a shift in focus.

Chapter 4

LISTEN TO THE MORE SOFT AND VULNERABLE FEELINGS THAT LIE BENEATH ANGER

I often hear clients cite self-help books in which they have read that it is healthy to express their anger. And when they follow that advice, some of them end up in conflicts that make them even angrier than they were before. As a fundamental rule, when you express your anger to someone you can be sure that you will be initiating a feeling of anger in them as well. Anger is contagious.

In some instances this works just fine. Perhaps the two of you just need to have a healthy argument to clear the air and you can laugh at it afterwards. In other instances things may get much worse when you express your anger.

Up until recently it was believed that you could get rid of your anger by expressing it in various ways, as, for example, hitting a pillow. However, if you make aggressive movements with your body, you are actually doing the exact opposite; that is, you are sustaining your anger or, even worse, you are intensifying it. Talking to someone about it or doing a relaxation exercise works much better.

Soft and vulnerable feelings

When it comes to anger, it is often the case that it is actually covering up more feelings of vulnerability. If you are able to get in touch with those underlying feelings you will end up with a different kind of energy, one that allows for a greater sense of transition and healing.

Sometimes anger is the primary emotion, in which case it is usually a good idea to express it. However, in my experience I have found that anger is usually secondary. When anger is a secondary emotion it constitutes a comparatively superficial emotional layer that is usually protecting deeper and more essential feelings lying below the surface and which make more sense in terms of the situation.

Primary and secondary anger in various situations

There are a variety of reasons why anger arises. Once you have determined the triggering factor, you will be better able to find a suitable way of confronting your anger because you will discover that you have different needs, depending on what the anger derives from. There are in fact four main categories of reasons why anger arises:

1. Others say or do something that hurts your vanity. In my experience, this is the most common reason why anger arises. Your self-image has taken a blow.

2. Others offer you intimacy or compassion which you either do not wish for or do not dare to receive at the moment. The anger or irritation is a form of self-protection that is initiated almost automatically as a defence mechanism against the intimacy that is being offered to you.

3. The action of others is in conflict with your values or maxims.

4. Something occurs or is happening that is the opposite of what you wish for or want.

These categories are further elaborated below.

1. Self-image is threatened

Anger that is due to hurt vanity is called narcissistic anger. When your self-image has taken a blow you will typically want to express how angry you are over what the other party said or did, or even get back at the person, just like children tend to do when they say, 'If I am, then so are you,' when they get criticised. You will most likely also want to come up with a lot of explanations, the purpose of which is really to alter the impression the other person now has of you. None of the methods work! Neither expressing your anger nor attacking the other person will change their impression of you, and certainly not for the better. The explanations won't either. On the contrary, they may irritate the other person, who probably just wants to be able to trust his or her own intuitions and maintain their own view of you without too much outside interference.

Take, for example, Hans who says to his wife, Inga, 'Aren't you a little lazy?' whereupon she registers her own anger and her desire to respond by giving a lot of explanations of how much she actually manages to get done. When that doesn't work it is because in this case anger is secondary, and lying beneath that anger are probably two other emotions that are more vulnerable in nature.

One is the sorrow in not being seen in the way that she would like to be seen, in which case it would be appropriate for her to express this by saying, for example, 'I'm sorry that you perceive me that way,' and perhaps adding, 'That is not how I perceive myself.' To which he might respond, 'How do you see yourself then?' which would allow her to give her explanations now that Hans has expressed a willingness to listen to her.

The other feeling which may lie below narcissistic anger is fear or anxiety. In Inga's case, for example, she may ask herself whether he will continue to want to live together with her if he sees her that way, or does she risk being abandoned by him? Whether or not there is any basis for her having this fear is something which she can look into by asking, 'When you experience me in this way, does that mean you like me less?' to which he may respond, 'No, not at all, I think it's wonderful that you are so good at enjoying life while I'm at work because it means that you will be more relaxed and happy when I come home.' Then both her anger and fear will immediately dissipate, which is particularly beneficial for someone who is sensitive. Having an argument in this instance would be a waste of time.

If the situation is the opposite and you are the one who has said or done something which has initiated a narcissistic form of anger in the other person, you can choose to focus on the underlying sorrow or fear instead of on the anger. If you can show the other person that you are capable of seeing them in a positive light, and he or she is able to recognise themselves in the things you say, it will help to calm the situation down.

Let's say that I have said to the other person that I think he looks as though he is particularly sensitive or vulnerable, and he responds by getting angry. This is either because it is wrong or because he does not want to be perceived in that way, perhaps because he associates sensitivity with weakness and has learned that he has to be 'cool' in order not to be abandoned.

Instead of starting an argument over it, the first thing I will do is be open to the possibility that I may be wrong. And then I would say something along the lines that I perceive it as a strength if someone dares to show their feelings and that I perceive him as being a strong person in many ways as well as being a pleasant person to be in the company of. In that way I am both pacifying his fear and soothing his pain. It may be that inwardly I now perceive him as even more vulnerable, but I will keep that to myself. He may someday be better able to handle and accept that aspect of himself.

I could have chosen instead to express my irritation over having to be confronted with his anger just because I had shared my perception of him by talking about how unpleasant an experience this had been for me. But then I would just have been feeding further into the fear and sorrow lying just below his anger, which would merely have made his anger increase.

Does this mean that I will be unable to ever express my irritation? I may mention it at some point when things have settled down, or write about it in my diary. Being able to accept your own feelings without necessarily having to immediately express them is, fortunately, something most of us get better at with age; this is a good thing because it saves us from getting into too many conflicts and from having to confront others' anger or hurt feelings in situations which could have ended peacefully if we had only kept our immediate reactions to ourselves. Though keeping your feelings to yourself is not always the best thing to do and may give rise to other problems, it is always a good thing to have had the possibility to choose.

Your reaction depends on whether the hurtful comments are being directed at your person or your actions. That is, whether it is your actions the other person doesn't approve of or whether it is you as a person. If it is your behaviour which you think is being criticised you have the option to change it. For example: your colleague tells you that you are not getting enough done at your job. If you agree with him and can see that you are doing less than he is and at the same time have the possibility to become more efficient, then you have the option to change your behaviour. You may even become more satisfied with yourself as a result.

2. Need for self-protection

One example could be when Lone comes home to her husband, Per, after she has been passed over for a promotion. She is vulnerable and is not ready to confront her feelings of disappointment. Instead, she busies herself in the kitchen and when Per tries to put his arms around her she snaps at him and criticises his food shopping.

Here anger is again secondary. It is either a cover-up or a form of protection. It is alright not to want to experience your feelings, and it is also a really good idea to say so out loud. For example, you could say, 'Right now I don't feel like experiencing or sensing my feelings and I can best distance myself from them if I also distance myself from you,' and possibly adding, 'It has nothing to do with you, and I will let you know when I am ready to talk about it.'

There is also the possibility that you experience your anger as being almost a forced reaction which you do not have full control over. Perhaps you wish for more intimacy and deep down don't really want for there to be so much distance which your, possibly explosive, anger creates between you and other people. In that case, I recommend that you talk with a professional therapist about it. It is a waste of energy having to be distanced from other people if you don't want to be, and it is something that can be overcome with professional help.

3. Maxims or values have taken a blow

When you react with anger to something that others have done it may have to do with maxims. Aside from the laws and rules that society delegates, all people have a certain set of rules or maxims, which they have either inherited from their parents or created themselves and which they follow. Most people are not fully aware of their own maxims and may benefit from focusing on them.

The other person may do something which you have forbidden yourself from doing. For example, I can get irritated over people who talk incessantly and who seemingly aren't too concerned as to whether or not what they are saying is of any interest to other people. There are two ways that I can work with this: I can try to get the other person to change his or her behaviour or I can change my own. In this case, I might consider whether I should let myself talk just a little bit more spontaneously without feeling that I have to constantly take into consideration the extent to which the other person finds what I'm saying interesting or not.

If you hold yourself to very high standards you will become easily irritated at others who perhaps allow themselves to be more laid back. It might be a good idea to become aware of your own maxims and then determine whether some of them could be modified.

It is a different story, however, when it comes to values. If one of your values is that you have to protect and care for nature and wild animals you will probably get angry when you see people pouring poison into the environment. In such a case I would not recommend taking a more relaxed attitude toward pesticides. On the contrary, your sense of well-being will increase if you are fighting for your values by, for example, becoming an active member of an interest group that has the same set of values as you have.

4. Discrepancy with wishes

In situations that fall under this category something is going on that bothers you but it is not due to a hurt sense of pride, or that others are getting too close to you or are acting contrary to your maxims or values. In other words, this category consists of occurrences that go against what you want and desire and at the same time excludes the other three categories. Some examples might be:

~ You experience something happening that delays or hinders you from reaching your destination (puts a spanner in the works).

~ You do not get what you wished for (disappointment, which is a mixed feeling that may, to a large extent, consist of anger; read about mixed feelings in Chapter 1).

~ People cross your boundaries, move your things around or dance too intimately with your partner. The latter may awaken a kind of territorial anger that can clearly be seen in animals.

In all the situations above anger is primary. It is as though anger is created to mark boundaries and do away with hindrances. For example, when you discover that your neighbour has parked in front of your garage you can probably sense your irritation increasing like rising energy and you start preparing yourself to take action. You can choose to tell your neighbour how angry you are over it and how inconsiderate you think it is of him. Expressing your anger can really leave you with a great feeling. It is as though your whole system is letting out a big sigh of relief. Unfortunately that sense of joy is usually short-lived because you can be sure that, when you give out your anger to someone, you will be getting it right back again. Your neighbour will in all probability express just how unpleasant it is to be confronted in that way.

I usually recommend to my clients and course participants that they express their anger in the form of a wish instead. If you are angry it really means you have a wish that isn't being fulfilled at the moment. If you are aware of what the wish is and dare to express it instead of your anger, you will most likely end up getting better results. So you could, for example, say to your neighbour, 'I would really appreciate it if you parked your car about four feet to the left of my garage. That way it will be easier for me to get my car out.' The neighbour will most likely be happy to do that.

Or if there is a colleague who has borrowed your computer without your permission you might say, 'I would appreciate it if next time you asked whether you can borrow my computer. That way I can get a chance to save all my data and ensure that nothing gets erased.' This wish, too, will most likely be fulfilled without any problem.

When something is going on that opposes your wishes, there is also another possibility apart from expressing your wish in an attempt to change the situation. You can choose to let go of wanting the wish to be fulfilled. When you let go of a struggle, anger turns into sorrow. There is a greater possibility for a sense of life and movement to emerge in sorrow, as opposed to in anger. Sorrow is not static but grows smaller over time and usually disappears entirely after either a short or long period of time. After that you will probably discover other wishes and possibilities.

For example, suppose that the colleague who borrows your computer without asking first refuses to fulfil your wish of being asked beforehand whether he can borrow it. You can put up a fight or you can let go and prepare yourself for a new situation. It would of course be disappointing if you didn't get what you initially wished for, but after a while you will probably become used to the new situation and to the habit of saving all of your work before leaving your workplace.

When anger is secondary it can be beneficial to relate to the more vulnerable feelings lying below the surface. In the instances where anger is primary it may be more advantageous for you to express it in the form of a wish. Or you can choose to let go. Read more about the various possibilities of letting go later in the chapter.

. . . .

Model 1 summarises the four categories of reason why anger arises, together with corresponding tools for dealing with them. The four segments from the diagram are referred to as 'tool boxes' in the explanations that follow.

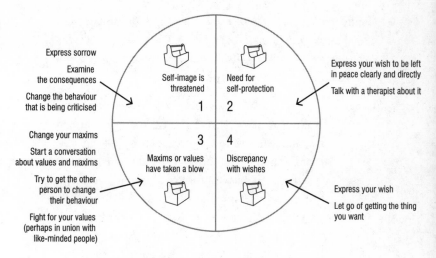

Model 1: The four categories of reason for anger,
with corresponding tools for dealing with them

Some situations fall under several categories

Example A

Let's say your friend calls off an engagement with you at very short notice. This type of situation first and foremost belongs under the fourth category, 'Discrepancy with wishes'.

But even if you are relieved (and therefore there is no discrepancy with wishes) because, let's say, you really didn't have the energy for the visit, there may still be something that has rubbed off from the other categories. Perhaps you have a maxim that prohibits you from calling off engagements, making you think that your friend's action was wrong (Category 3). Perhaps your self-image has taken a blow as well because you don't feel respected or appreciated by your friend when he breaks off his engagement with you, especially if he doesn't make a real apology (Category 1).

If the situation falls under several categories, you have more tool boxes to choose from:

~ *Tools from box 1 (your self-image has taken a blow):* Examine whether there is any reason for you to feel that you are less appreciated by asking your friend whether he often calls off engagements or whether it has anything to do with you. And if it becomes apparent that he called off the engagement because he does not prioritise your friendship, you can express your sorrow by saying, 'I am sorry that I do not mean more to you,' or, 'I wish that you prioritised me more highly.'

~ *Tools from box 3 (values or maxims):* Consider whether you can work with your maxim and make it less strict. If it sounds anything like, 'You may never call off an appointment or engagement,' perhaps you can change it to, 'You may only call off an engagement if you have a really good reason to do so.' However, you may also be satisfied with your rule and therefore do not wish to change it.

You can start the conversation by telling your friend about your maxims or values and ask about his. Maybe the two of you will end up determining that your rules and values differ. Still, talking about the rules may result in the two of you having a better understanding of one another's reactions.

You can also try changing your friend's behaviour by making a direct request, such as, 'It is important to me that I can count on it if I make plans with my friends. If you need to change our plans another time I would like to know as soon as possible.'

~ *Tools from box 4 (discrepancy with wishes):* Hold on to what you wish for by expressing it – by saying, for example, 'I would appreciate it if you would reconsider your decision about calling it off. I was looking forward to seeing you and I think we could have a really nice time together.'

If the person is unable to alter the cancellation and you discover that your friend really doesn't prioritise you, you may want to consider whether the relationship is valuable enough for you to want to keep it, because it would seem that there is a price to pay for it, namely, that your friend will call off any plans he made with you if he gets an invitation from someone he prioritises more. Or you may let go of trying to get your friend to change his behaviour and choose to put up with it instead because you don't want to lose him.

In most situations you would probably start by expressing your wish in the hope that something might change. And if it can't, you will sometimes have to choose to let go of the relationship or any hope you may have had that it would change. However, there may also be instances in which you are able to determine from the start that either the situation is unalterable or that the consequences will be too bothersome if you try to change it and so you choose to let go of it without first expressing your wish.

If you find your friend to be a particularly giving or interesting person, you will probably choose to let go of changing the situation and instead get used to the idea of having to pay a price for it. If you find that you don't consider him to be all that valuable, perhaps you should give him an ultimatum: either he keeps his word when you make plans together or you won't make any more with him.

The shaded area in Model 2 indicates the tools used for dealing with anger in this example. The size of the shaded areas reflects the importance of the particular tool box.

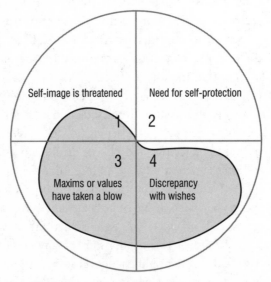

Model 2: The shaded area indicates the tools used for dealing with anger in Example A

Example B

We now look at another example where several categories are simultaneously at play.

Suppose your neighbour says to you that you are being unfair. Your self-image gets a blow, which would be Category 1. If he doesn't say it to you in a calm voice, but as he snaps at you, or shouts or screams and says it in front of people witnessing the situation, it probably also belongs to Category 4 (discrepancy with wishes) and maybe Category 3 (values or maxims).

In this case you can get tools from several different boxes:

~ *Tools from box 1 (self-image is threatened):* Express your sorrow by saying, for example, 'I'm sorry that you think I'm being unreasonable.' You might add, 'Maybe you are right,' or 'That's not how I see it.'

  You can also examine what it would mean for your relationship in the future by saying, 'I hope this doesn't mean that we can't walk together to the soccer games at the stadium.'

~ *Tools from box 3 (values or maxims):* You can choose to alter your maxim if it's something like, 'You are not allowed to bother others by yelling or snapping at them,' or, 'If you want to confront someone, do it when there are just the two of you and not in public.' It is probably more likely that you will tell your neighbour about your values, and ask him to respect your boundaries for how you want to be spoken to and how you don't.

~ *Tools from box 4 (discrepancy with wishes):* You can again choose to express your wish to be spoken to with respect.

You can also choose to let go of changing your neighbour's way of speaking to you. The best thing may be to bear with him if, for example, he is senile or has a mental illness or a functional disorder which makes him behave in a socially awkward way.

The shaded area in Model 3 indicates the tools used in this example.

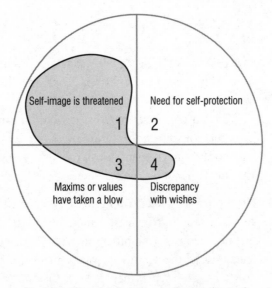

Model 3: The shaded area indicates the tools used for dealing with anger in Example B

When anger is covering up a sense of helplessness and sorrow

As mentioned before, it is often the case that the anger we seem to be experiencing is covering up other feelings which happen to be much more constructive to work with. Within these feelings there is often a new path that lies hidden, one that can lead us to new places where we are more authentic, vital and happy. Anger has a tendency to lie on the topmost layer beneath which a host of emotions may lie hidden, which you may not be entirely aware of because anger tends to fill up most of the space.

Within anger there is a hidden hope that reality can be altered. Anger is a strong form of energy which is created to remove obstacles or hindrances. And to struggle with the thing that you want to change. As long as you are angry, then there is something which you are fighting to change, regardless of whether or not you are aware if it.

The problem is when you are fighting for something that cannot be changed. For example, if you are angry with your partner because you are hoping that he will change his fundamental personality traits if you scold or correct him enough times, then you are making life bitter for not only your partner but also yourself. And for no good reason. Fundamental personality traits are seldom alterable.

Or if you continue to be angry at your elderly parents. As long as you are angry there is something you fight for. You may not be aware of it yourself but within anger a sense of hope lies hidden, a hope that what has happened can somehow be undone: that you in some miraculous way can still attain the things you didn't get when you were a child; or at least some form of compensation; that Mum or Dad will change at the very end and that you can live happily ever after, like in the fairy tales.

When you don't want to be a part of reality

We are often angry until we become strong enough to face our loss and accept reality as it is. The day you dare to let go of a hopeless battle, anger will become a sorrow. And sorrow, as opposed to anger, has the advantage of appealing to other people's sense of compassion. You will receive help. Aside from that, there is a sense of movement in sorrow. A healthy form of sorrow will last for a certain amount of time until you have 'mourned' yourself free of your loss and are ready to dry your eyes and seek new possibilities. Anger, on the other hand, may turn into bitterness and last for the rest of your life.

The pattern with anger, where a sense of hope lies hidden, plays out in many relationships, as for example with ex-partners, siblings or employees. If you become aware of the hope and the battle taking place you will be better able to find your way so that you can move forward. If you can find hope in your anger, and either change reality wherever possible or let go of hope and 'mourn' yourself free, you are ready to start a new life.

When you have mourned your way through whatever it is you didn't get in your childhood or, for example, from your partner, you will better be able to see your parents and others for who they really are, with all their strengths and limitations just like yourself. And even though you can never get a new childhood or turn back time and start your love relationship over again, the relationships can still change in nature once you stop trying to force out of others the things that they don't have, and let go of your wish to change reality and other people.

If you yourself encounter anger coming from, for example, your adult children, you can include powerlessness in the conversation by saying, for example, 'I wish I could have given you a new childhood.' Or to your friend who claims that you ruined his birthday by going home early, you could say, 'I wish I had been able to act differently.'

From 'should' to 'wish': from anger to sorrow

'Should' is a word that is good to use when you are moralising. You can moralise either to yourself or to others. 'I should have had more energy for my children' is an example of a moral judgment you can make of yourself. You turn the anger inwards and direct it at yourself.

You can also raise a moralising finger at someone else: 'You should have thought more about me,' or even worse, 'After everything I've done for you, you ought to at least show just a little gratitude.' If you like getting internally worked up over something, you can start by thinking in 'moral' terms, in relation either to yourself or to others.

The difference between wishes and hope

You can distinguish between wishes and hope. Hope should comply with reality. If what you are hoping for exists partially in a fairy-tale world, you may end up wasting a lot of time and energy on something which, when it comes down to it, is really dead. An example could be the wife who remains in a loveless marriage in the hope that her husband one day will change his fundamental personality traits. It would serve her much better to let go of that hope. Without having the hope that her husband will change, she can better relate to the reality of her actual situation and decide whether she is willing to accept it or needs to remove herself from it.

Wishes are a different story. You can easily wish for something that is entirely unrealistic; for example, that a deceased loved one will return just for one moment. You do not decide yourself what it is you wish for deep down. Whether you prefer yellow as opposed to blue colours is not something you can decide for yourself but is something you discover by listening to your inner self. In a way, you could say that you are your wishes.

Whenever I want to discover who a person is, I'll ask what it is he or she wishes for. The answer will tell me a lot about the person.

Sensing your wishes is to be close to yourself. When you dare to sense and accept your wishes in the present moment, you are being authentically intimate. And if at the same time you are open to listening to the wishes of other people, a connection of very high quality may emerge.

Wishes cannot be wrong

You are not the master of your wishes. You can try to repress them, but repressions come with a price which doesn't pay off in the end. The price you pay for repressing your wishes is a loss of vitality, and having a feeling of meaninglessness or just a general sense of grey sadness.

Wishes are full of life. It can hurt to feel your wishes if you are living a life that is very different from how you wish it could be. When you are feeling what your wishes are, you will be in contact with your sorrow and with your deeper self. I myself prefer to maintain a good connection with my sorrow so in that way I can sense that I am alive, as opposed to experiencing the empty, flat sensation that comes from putting a lid on too many painful realisations.

When you are moralising to yourself or others, then you are in contact with your anger, which you are either directing outward or inward. When you are in contact with your wish, you will feel pain if it cannot be fulfilled and joy if it can.

Saying to yourself, 'I ought to be able to handle the same things everyone else can,' can be changed to, 'I wish I could handle the same things.' In the latter sentence, the sense of blame has been removed and there is more room for sorrow. And, 'You ought to have helped me some more,' can be changed to, 'I wish you had helped me some more,' or even more to the point, 'I missed your help.'

I hope that you as the reader can sense how you are reaching completely different vibrations when you are speaking on the basis of a wish, as opposed to when you are moralising and using the word 'should'. Try taking one of your typical judgments about yourself or others and reformulate it to 'I wish' or 'I miss' and then feel the change that takes place inside of you. More peace will come, however sorrowful it may be.

Anger is usually a surface layer. Many people remain in a state of anger a lot longer rather than allow themselves to move down into the more vulnerable feelings. There may be several reasons for this: perhaps you are unable to accommodate the sorrow lying under the anger; or maybe you cannot stand the feeling of powerlessness you get from having to acknowledge the fact that there is something that you cannot attain and that you have no influence over. When you are in a state of anger, it is a sign that there is something you are fighting for. The more you fight, the less you need to feel.

For some people it feels better to direct their feeling of anger at old, failed relationships rather than accept what happened in the past. But the past cannot be changed! You have the scars, and you will have to live with the loss associated with them. The day you can accept this as reality is the day your anger will turn to sorrow.

And there is a healing aspect to sorrow. Sorrow is a process that needs time. When you are experiencing sorrow it is much easier for you to receive love from other people than when you are angry. When you are angry, the chance of someone offering you compassion is much less. Anger creates distance, whereas sorrow calls on compassion.

Summary

If your anger arises because your boundaries have been crossed you can express it as a wish. If you are accustomed to expressing your anger in such situations, a new way for you may be to find the wish that lies hidden within the anger and say something about it instead.

If your or someone else's anger is really covering up other, more vulnerable, feelings, a much better connection will arise from talking about them, if possible. If instead of mentioning your anger you talk about your feeling of helplessness, anxiety or sorrow you will find a new way or path that will allow for a greater sense of warmth in your relationships.

Chapter 5

SAY WHAT YOU WISH FOR AND WANT

If you don't like conflicts it can be tempting to never express anything negative and just pretend that everything is fine. You may say to yourself that it isn't so important anyway. If you experience something happening that you don't like, it is a matter of finding a middle ground between extreme positions. One extreme would be to give the other party a good scolding. The other would be to blame yourself. Somewhere in between those two scenarios lies the possibility to say something about yourself. And it should, as far as possible, be said as a statement, as a neutral piece of information about what you are registering or sensing.

That is to say, it should not sound like, 'You just managed to ruin my mood,' nor, 'I'm always much too sensitive.' Below are some examples of statements:

'When you look at me that way it gives me a nervous stomach.'

'I wish that you would say something nice to me now.'

'I would rather have salad than pickles.'

'It is important to me that I can rely on the plans we make together.'

The more clearly you express what you prefer and want, the more clearly you will come across in your connection with the other person. Clear boundaries create good connections. The more you dare to show who you are, the deeper your connections will be.

Even though in the short term, especially if you don't like anger, it is easier to say to yourself that it really doesn't matter, in the long term it is a bad idea. If you never dare to say negative things you risk that your relationships will always remain superficial and ultimately unsatisfying to you.

If you don't stand your ground in situations where it would be appropriate to do so, it may be due to low self-esteem:

I have often been told that I should stop putting up with things and instead bang my fist on the table and gain some respect. And I have tried to follow this well-meaning piece of advice, but every time I was about to raise my voice it would break and become soft, thin and hoarse.

I see now that it had to do with my having low self-esteem. Deep down I was insecure as to whether I had any right to even exist in the world. I felt that I was wrong and that I was someone who ought to really be thankful for even being allowed to be a part of the human community. And on top of that I couldn't really afford to be a bother. Whenever I was about to express my anger, I would simply get scared. It wasn't because I couldn't feel the anger and it wasn't because I didn't know how to make myself heard.

(Jens, 45 years old)

A man like Jens does not have a need to work with his anger, even though that was what he had been encouraged to do by various parties. What he does need to work with is his self-esteem.

If saying what you want or don't want doesn't work

Some people think that they won't get heard because they aren't raising their voices. I believe that within this belief it is possible to find the residue of past experiences. When we were babies it was the only thing we could do. If Mum and Dad didn't remove whatever it was that was causing us discomfort, it was just a matter of screaming a little louder and making life a nuisance for them in various ways until they came to rectify it.

This is a strategy the remains of which I sometimes see in couples' conflicts. Perhaps you are familiar with the desire to make life difficult for your partner in the hope that that way he will understand that he needs to do something to remove your frustrations. And you may not even be entirely aware of what it is he needs to do. This strategy worked well once but is fatal once you become an adult. As grown-ups, if we bother others with our frustrations the outcome is usually not good; in fact, we often find that we do not get the things we want, but what we do get is more unpleasantness. A calm and composed 'No' or 'I would rather not' or 'I am not OK with that' works better than raging anger.

And in the situations where it doesn't work just to nicely and calmly state what you want or don't want, raging anger won't do either. Because this usually means that it is a situation which cannot be altered owing to the fact that the person from whom you want something either does not have it or is not willing or able to provide it.

If you have stated what you don't want and the situation persists, it can sometimes help to set consequences for certain actions, such as, for example, 'Next time you are too late I won't wait for you.'

Summary

If you inform your surroundings of what it is you wish for and want you will be seen in a much clearer light. Saying your wishes out loud is a way of respecting yourself. Even though things can't always turn out the way you wished for, you will probably feel better about having expressed your wish, as opposed to keeping quiet about it.

If you have said 'no' to something you did not want to partake in and it continues to persist, it rarely helps to raise your voice about it. Perhaps a new way or path for you would be to set consequences for the things that happen and show through your actions that you mean what you say.

Chapter 6

RESIST BEING 'SAD' OR EMBRACE IT ENTIRELY

When the things that you wish for and want to do cannot become a part of reality, you will experience having a feeling of sadness.

You can go against that feeling of being sad by shifting your focus to something pleasant. One way of doing this is by making a list of all the positive things various people have said to you or about you through your whole life. For a period of time, you can make a daily habit of reminding yourself of at least one positive statement that has been made about you. Find more positive statements on your own.

Starting to go to activities that you enjoy is another way of improving your mood. And even if you cannot sense exactly what it is you feel like doing, still try and see if you can engage yourself with something that you might like doing. You can read more about increasing your happiness in Chapter 11.

If you tend to mope around a lot for longer periods of time while concentrating on finding out what it is you are sad about, then activities that improve your mood may be the way to go for you. Perhaps you have tried to find the root of the trouble but to no avail and have therefore mulled over it for too long. There is nothing wrong with trying to find the root of your troubles. You just need to be aware of the fact that you are initiating a lot of thoughts pertaining to the problem, which may make you feel gloomy, and that the root of a problem cannot always be found; and even if it can, knowing what it is does not always change things all that much. Perhaps in your eagerness to find the root of the problem you end up thinking too much in terms of problems and not enough in terms of strengths and resources.

If you are really good at focusing on your strengths and thinking positively but still without your feelings of sadness diminishing, a new approach for you may be to do the opposite: fully embrace being sad and allow yourself to cry it all out.

Be aware of the fact that there are two forms of crying, which we will refer to as a 'calling-out cry' and a 'letting-go cry'. Whereas anger is the feeling that is mostly associated with a sense of struggle, being sad is more associated with letting go.

Calling out

Regressive calling-out cry

If, at this very moment, you feel unable either to struggle or let go, you are probably experiencing regressive sadness.

Regression means that you go back to using a specific strategy which was pivotal in an earlier phase of development. For example, when a child who has become potty-trained starts to wet his bed at night again, we call that regression. The cause may be due to the fact that the child is experiencing a challenge of some sort, such as, for example, having a new sibling or starting in day care.

We regress when we are no longer able to handle the challenges we face and thereby become nervous. The regressive form of crying is an expression of anxiety, not sadness. The thoughts that are connected with regressive crying may sound something like, 'I can't stand it any more, help me.'

A client explains: 'Sometimes I start to cry when I am very angry. Typically, just as I am about to express utter rage, my voice will crack and turn small and the sound that comes out is more of a hissing sound as opposed to the roar I thought was on its way.' This is a phenomenon that many women are familiar with.

Many men become confused when their otherwise very angry girlfriend starts crying. They have learned that when a woman cries you have to be nice to them, making it hard for them to retain their own anger. Some men think that crying is something women do purposefully to put pressure on others. But it usually isn't. It is a regression which most women wish they could dismiss. But she becomes too scared and then the regression emerges.

When women become more scared of anger than men it is usually due to the fact that women are more likely to be brought up to think that anger is bad. She may have experienced being ostracised whenever she was angry: 'Go into your room and stay there until you know how to behave again.' So when she is about to express strong anger, her abandonment fear becomes so strong that she regresses.

Men have also had similar experiences in their childhood. However, it is as though anger is more accepted in little boys than in little girls. On the other hand, little boys may have heard that only sissies cry. It is for this reason that it is more seldom that men regress when experiencing strong anger.

Another example of a calling-out cry may be seen with widows and widowers during the first phase of their loss. As long as they can't cope with their own emotional reaction to the loss, which they typically can't in the beginning, they will mainly exhibit this form of crying.

Calling out for care

On the positive side, a calling-out cry sends a certain signal which most of us instinctively have a positive reaction to. The signal indicates, 'Give me care.' And if you haven't had too many bad experiences with others' crying and feel comfortable about your own, the tears of others will then awaken your need to show them compassion and in that way you help them in a completely natural way.

It jars my ears when I hear someone say that being sad is a negative feeling, because a sense of intimacy may emerge as a result of tears. Perhaps you are familiar with the phenomenon of moving closer to and affectionately caressing the person who is crying.

Some people do not want to admit that they have a longing for compassion. They have learned that it is best to look out for themselves and not burden others. Sometimes I will encounter a client who claims that he is fine handling something on his own as a tear rolls down his cheek. I see the tear as an expression of the client's more authentic and susceptible side that has been repressed but which is sending out an emergency signal by way of the tear.

When you become touched

Some people become touched when they see a movie or listen to another person's story. I sometimes become touched while sitting and listening to a patient. Most often I choose to say something about my moved state. In my experience, doing this helps strengthen the client's sense that we are sharing something and that we are experiencing something joyful or difficult together.

A number of people think it is embarrassing when they are moved. A typical example would be that someone says something nice about you or gives you a present, and you get tears in your eyes and may choke up. The tears reveal how much it means to you and how much you have longed for someone to give you that. If the sensation of being moved or touched by something feels dangerous it may be because it is only the tip of the iceberg. And beneath that there may be an enormous sense of need as well as a powerful and unhappy longing for love.

To be touched and to allow yourself to be moved by something is a sign of health. It is a form of contact which you express by showing the other person that what is happening right now is of significance. Most people become happy to see someone being moved because they gave them a present or compliment.

When is the calling-out cry meaningful?

A calling-out cry is meaningful when you are together with others. I think it is healthy to sometimes allow yourself to regress, become very small inside and let others take over, console and support you. At best, you will, after a short while, and with regained strength, be once again ready to use your adult strategies.

When you are alone, however, no one is going to hear your calling anyway, so in that situation it is best to go for a walk or start occupying yourself with something that usually gives you joy and energy.

You have probably heard that it is healthy to cry. In Denmark there is an old proverb:

> And if you have wept
> your eyes to weariness
> it will lighten your heart.

However, that does not apply to the regressive calling-out cry because there is nothing healthy about it if you are crying all alone. It can last for days and you risk developing a headache instead of experiencing a form of release. Maybe it's the best you can do for yourself at the moment. But there is no reason to practise it in the belief that it is healthy.

If you are able to shift away from the regressive calling-out cry and over to the kind of crying that gives you a sense of release (which I will describe shortly), you will have a clearer experience of your sorrow being in a form of 'process'. You can initiate the shift yourself by writing a farewell letter. Read more about this later on in the chapter and in Appendix 1.

Letting go, and the crying that accompanies it

The feeling of being sad derives from an experience of loss. There is something you have lost or something that you wish you had right now but don't. It doesn't have to be anything big. Also, the loss of hope or a specific dream may initiate a sense of mourning.

The moment you see your loss for what it is you will start to cry, either through flowing tears or sobs that will make your whole body shake. Some people experience this form of crying, which seldom lasts more than 5–6 minutes, as being just as liberating and stress-relieving as an orgasm.

Some people report having a sense that there is a lump in their throat and a need to cry but they feel as though there is something stopping them from crying. It is like a wave that does not break. For some people it is easiest to let go when they are together with people they feel safe with. For others the best thing is to be alone. If you are of the latter category and just need that extra 'small push' that will help you to let go, you can try the following, which I call 'Be your own good parent'.

Be your own good parent

We have all had a personal mother and father figure or other caregivers, with all the resources and limitations that people typically have. At the same time, we also have an idea of what the ultimately good parent is like, the one who fully understands and accepts all our feelings, who loves us unconditionally and always says exactly what we need to hear.

Talk to yourself as though you are that ultimately good parent. When I do it, for example, it sounds something like this: 'Sweet Ilse, it is a shame that things didn't go as you had hoped they would. You have fought so hard to get this thing, and you just wanted it so very much...' And then I describe as precisely as I possibly can what it is I had hoped for and how wonderful it would have been had it manifested. Then all the tears come up automatically of themselves, and I can let go.

If, at the same time, you embrace yourself or caress yourself affectionately on your arms, the feeling will be intensified. But this method is not always enough to truly break the wave, which I discuss next.

Resistance to letting go

Imagine an empty marmalade jar hanging upside down from a string in mid-air. A fly has become stuck in there and is desperately flying in circles to escape from the top of the glass, which is impossible. The only means of escape is down through the opening of the jar. But it is so intent on flying upward that it continues to stressfully fly in circles at the very top instead of allowing itself to fall a few centimetres downward and thereby gain freedom.

I recognise that sense of resistance to allowing myself to fall deep within myself in order to face something heavy and difficult. So I sometimes end up living with inner stress for a long period of time before finally allowing myself to surrender and let go, falling downward back to myself.

Knowing that I am capable of letting go and returning home gives me greater courage to get involved with people and things that I risk losing in the long run.

Some people get stronger when they experience great sorrow because they learn that you can mourn yourself through deep pain. And having that knowledge makes life less dangerous. Others never mourn something entirely through and so carry the burden of a sorrow that they either completely or partially have tried to avoid maybe for the rest of their lives. The symptoms of avoided sorrow may resemble those seen in post-traumatic stress disorder (PTSD) or personality disorders. And the avoided sorrow may result in a depression.

If your relation to the one you have loved was complicated, the sorrow will be heavier. Perhaps you have wondered why the sorrow was great even though you got very little from your lost one. But people who have had a close, warm and uncomplicated relationship have a much easier time letting go. They have all the good memories to live off.

If your relationship was ambivalent and you never got what you needed out of it in order to be whole, it will be harder to let go of it. You are faced with having to say good-bye not only to the person, but also to everything you never received and to the last hope that you might someday still get it from the person. Just as it can be difficult to abandon unfinished work, it can also be difficult to have to abandon a relationship that never worked.

Share your sorrow

When survivors of a death, or people who have faced a divorce, continue to get stuck in feelings of anger or bitterness through many years, it may be a sign that they are unable to cope with their own emotional response to the loss. In order to be able to deal with a strong emotional response reaction to something, a person's 'I' must be strong enough to bear it, and there must also be at least one caring person who can support and help the person with accepting the loss and accommodating the feeling of helplessness and sorrow that naturally tend to follow.

If it is too hard to let go, it may be because you are still not strong enough to accept your emotional reaction to the loss and have still not recognised the full impact of the situation.

If that is the case, it is a good idea to share your experiences with a person who is good at listening and helping you to accommodate your emotions. They say that a sorrow that is shared is only half as heavy. But it is not insignificant who you choose as a helper. It must be someone who is both able and willing to help you accommodate your feelings, otherwise you won't experience it as a relief. On the contrary, you will most likely end up with a feeling of being frustrated and confused, which will leave you with a sense of being wrong.

That is why it is a good idea to look into whether the other person is ready before you get started. You could say, for example, 'I want to tell you about something that is very painful to me. Do you feel up to hearing it and could I tell it to you now, or would it be better at a different time?' If the person you are speaking with answers negatively or evasively, it may be because he or she has experienced a similar form of pain which he or she has repressed but which would come to the surface in the form of anxiety when you tell your story.

If there is no one in your network who is willing or able to share your pain with you, you can seek a professional. There can be a number of advantages to using an entirely neutral person whom you can choose never to see again. Be aware of the fact that having a title such as psychotherapist or psychologist is no guarantee that the person is able to accommodate other people's feelings. The emotional capacity to deal with other people's feelings requires the ability to contain one's own, as well as having the resources to take on such an endeavour for someone else. If you are unsure, you can make your own little test and start by talking about a time when you experienced something less painful and see how it feels. If it feels comfortable and your sorrow has become easier to bear, you can continue by describing something that was more painful.

Write a farewell letter

Whenever I have a client whom I can sense would benefit from letting go of something or other, I assign them the task of writing a farewell letter to whatever or whomever they need to let go of. The client gets a piece of paper with a list of questions for inspiration. You can find the list in Appendix 1, together with two example farewell letters. Perhaps writing such a farewell letter will help you to let go.

When you are going to say good-bye you should preferably be able to do so with a 'thank you'. For example, if you are going to say good-bye to cigarettes, you must thank them for all the pleasurable moments they have given you. If you are going to say good-bye to an old survival strategy, as for example always saying to yourself, 'I must always cope with everything myself,' you should first thank the strategy for all the help it has given you. It was probably very useful once, otherwise you wouldn't have made it yours. Perhaps it protected you from experiencing how little resources or competences your parents really had in bringing you up. And being an easy and accommodating child perhaps meant that you got the most that you could out of that relationship.

When you say good-bye to a person you should both thank them and wish them well in the future. The word 'farewell' does in fact mean that you hope they will 'fare well'; in other words we are wishing the one we are letting go of all the best in their continued journey in life. If you cannot send your best wishes to the person you are letting go of, then you have not truly let go of them yet.

When you have written the letter it is a good idea to read it aloud to someone you feel safe with, for it is a good idea to have a witness. If you don't know anybody whom you would feel safe reading the letter to, you can use an old oak tree. They are always willing to listen.

Many people write their farewell letters while weeping. You will probably experience your feelings at close hand and it will become clear to you just how significant the person you are writing to was in your life. When your feelings emerge, you can let them stream out in tears, something which often allows a person to experience a sense of release.

Anger and bitterness need to be transformed into letting-go sadness

If you have old anger or bitterness stored up within you, it is a good idea for your soul to let go of it. And that is exactly what you can use a farewell letter for. Be as precise as possible about what it is you want to let go of.

Perhaps it is to a greater extent a dream or specific image you have of yourself rather than an actual person. If writing the letter doesn't help, perhaps it is because it needs to have a different address on it. Perhaps the biggest loss is not so much the person, but more the dream you had about what your relationship together should have been like but never was. Or perhaps your greatest loss is the loss of social status that was connected with you being together with him or her, in which case you should write the letter to the dream or social status respectively.

Give yourself time to be sad

In our culture we do not have much patience for sorrow. People who are sad are often pressured to get back on track again as quickly as possible. But in that way you risk missing out on the possibility for growth that may be found when you allow yourself to have a period in your life where you slow down and allow your energy to become introverted.

In my experience, people who have been down for a period of time often return with a renewed sense of energy as well as new perspectives on things. It is as though they have spent the period spreading out all the pieces in their inner jigsaw puzzle and finding a new way to assemble them.

Perhaps you yourself, after a period of time where you have allowed yourself to feel your pain and think about your life and perhaps also about your death, have returned to a more active life again and discovered that some things have become simpler and easier for you. Perhaps you have also experienced that your sense of happiness can grow even deeper than before. There is a saying: 'Pain hollows out the basin of joy, which results in better room for joy.'

But there is, of course, a limit as to how much you need to suffer and for how long.

When we let go too soon

Just as you may waste possibilities by remaining in something, for example a relationship that would be better for you to let go of, the opposite may be true as well.

Perhaps you have given up taking a degree or other study that might not be so unattainable if you just started believing more in yourself. Or perhaps you have given up hope of getting a romantic partner before you have seriously considered all your possibilities.

If you are experiencing a great sense of frustration and fatigue in your life, it may be because you have given up on something that you can barely live without. It is quite possible that you can't even recall what it is. Perhaps you gave it up in the early stages of your life, before you had developed a language that could help you attain the specific form of attention you were seeking, because it became too painful for you to be rejected in your attempt to get it. And now you are longing for exactly that form of focus and attention which you never got and therefore don't exactly know what it is and, much less, how you can get it.

If that is the case, you need to go in another direction; that is, you must go from giving up to embracing the fight and the anger to find the energy you need to work on getting what it is you need.

The first step is to become completely clear on what it is you long for. A client once asked me in utter despair, 'How am I ever going to discover what it is I long for if I can't remember or sense it?'

It is, however, not as hard as it sounds. A longing that is repressed will often want to come out into the light of day. It may emerge in the form of anxiety. Or you might find traces of it in your envy or fantasies.

If you go to a therapist for a period of time it will also arise in connection with your relation to the therapist. And that is where you can get help to find the exact right words and practise asking for the things you want to have. That is, if you have the courage to be that honest.

A client who had been coming to me for almost a year told me one day, hesitantly, that she sensed a need to sit on my lap and be held. That sort of longing has no place being fulfilled in the therapist's office. But the longing needs to be accommodated and thoroughly examined and articulated as precisely as possible.

When she had rediscovered her longing which she had given up on at one time, her next challenge was to go out into the world and get what it was she needed. And it is important not to give up or let go of your longing again.

It is a fine balance in life to know when you should fight and when you should let go of something. If you are sufficiently flexible, you will discover that it constantly alternates. At one moment the best thing for you is to let go, whereas the next moment may present something else that needs to be fought for.

You will typically be better at one than the other. If you are a fighter who tends to stubbornly continue your battles, you probably need to practise letting go, and experience the freedom that comes with it.

Summary

There are various ways you can react if you sense that you are sad. You can speed up the struggle in getting what you want, if possible. There is no reason for crying over something that may still be possibly accessible to you. Usually the trick is to see the difference between what is possible and what is not. As in the words of the old serenity prayer:

> *God, grant me the serenity to accept*
> *the things I cannot change,*
> *the courage to change the things I can,*
> *and the wisdom to know the difference.*

If you have decided to let go because you have accepted that the situation cannot be altered or because the price for struggling for it is too high, you will become sad. And here, again, there are two ways to deal with it. You can resist your feeling by shifting your thoughts to something positive and do something you find pleasant. You can also go along with your feeling of sadness and find the compassion and care you need, go into the sorrow entirely and let your thoughts revolve around the thing you wish you had. Perhaps that way you will be able to find a sense of release and the courage to move on. It is advantageous to be able to do both so that you can alternate between the two.

I always encourage my clients who are melancholy to do the things that give them joy so that they can gather enough energy and strength to fully embrace their pain.

If you always tend to resist the things that hurt you in life, the new way or strategy for you may be to go straight into the heart of your pain and cry it all out. However, if you tend to always go into your dark feelings, you can perhaps find a new path by resisting them and finding something that gives you joy.

If one doesn't work, try the other. In time you will find your own flexible way, allowing you to resist and follow your feelings interchangeably.

Chapter 7

USE YOUR ENVY CONSTRUCTIVELY

When I hold lectures on emotions I like to spend a few minutes talking about envy. Often some members of the audience will experience an 'Aha' moment. That is because they have learned that this particular emotion is wrong and bad. And when they hear that there is, in fact, a positive aspect to it, some of them gain, perhaps for the first time in their lives, the courage to talk about envy, a feeling which they have secretly been tortured by.

Having feelings of envy is a torment and there is nothing you can do about it. You have not chosen them yourself. If you had had a choice, you would probably have chosen to live without them. The basic substance of envy consists of longing, need and unused talents. You get envious of the person who has or is doing some of the things you long for yourself.

Some people who go to see a therapist find themselves stuck in a grey sadness where they cannot sense or feel their own wishes. And when I ask them, 'What do you want?' they do not respond. They don't know. At this point I will typically ask them, 'When do you feel envious?' And it is in response to this question that we occasionally are able to find the key to a number of repressed wishes and longings.

My own decision to start a career as a psychotherapist started with envy. A friend of mine had a therapy clinic and every time she would talk about it I would practically be in pain. Due to this situation, I suffered from envy for a long time and was ashamed of the fact that I couldn't just be happy for her. I finally achieved atonement when I began taking the envy I was feeling seriously and quit my day job in order to take a chance on my talents and the career that I was so drawn to.

Envy contains important messages

Bent Falk, a Danish registered psychotherapist, author and theologian, calls envy a mine detector that directs us to our longings and unused talents.

Within envy lies a longing and, most probably, an unused talent. If you sense the longing to its fullest extent and, more specifically, dare to sense or feel exactly what it is you are longing for, a path to move forward will often emerge.

A client of mine, Jens, was envious of his wealthy cousin. As he put it, 'I can't strive to become that rich. It's simply not within my capability.' But sometimes a new path or road will emerge when you move down to a deeper layer within yourself. Because what exactly is it about wealth itself that is so wonderful?

For Jens it became apparent that there were two things. One was the freedom in not having to work so much. The other had to do with his self-image. He wanted to be perceived as being a lucky man.

He managed to acquire freedom by moving to a cheaper apartment and lowering his expenses on things which it turned out really weren't so important to him. He also managed to make an agreement with his employer about getting unpaid holiday and days off. And it turned out that he had a real talent for enjoying his newly acquired freedom.

When we examined his need to be perceived as a lucky man, it soon became apparent that there was a traumatic event behind it. At school, he was the most miserable child in the class because he had been bullied for many years. When his parents finally discovered this, they moved him to a different school. Since then he had preferred not to talk about the bullying, or think about it, and simply tried to forget it and live his life as though it had never occurred. But every time he had the experience of being unfortunate or unlucky, as when sitting next to his rich cousin, the same feeling of helplessness, loneliness and ostracism that he had experienced in the schoolyard would sneak up on him.

Once he had managed to work through the trauma he no longer felt the urge to see himself as being luckier or more fortunate than others. He could suddenly see the distance that such thinking creates. Now he just wanted to be completely normal, meet other people at eye level and enjoy the connection it creates in doing so.

The desire to destroy

Envy is a mixed feeling which includes several other basic feelings, sadness usually being the strongest of them. Included in sadness is the sorrow and absence of the thing you long for. Anger is also included in this to a greater or lesser degree. Perhaps you sense just a slight irritation when the other person speaks at length about the very thing you miss in your life. Or perhaps your pain grows to such an extent that you actually want to ruin the thing the other person has.

Feeling the need to destroy something is not a dangerous thing in itself. There is a long way from feeling such an impulse to actually acting on it, unless you are psychotic or under the influence of alcohol or drugs. I hope your values won't allow you to do anything like that. Accepting your desire to do evil does not increase the chance of your actually doing it, as many people think. On the contrary! The more aware you become of your feelings, the better able you will be at controlling your actions.

There is also an element of joy incorporated in envy since you are sensing and feeling just how happy the other person is and how happy you yourself would have been had you attained the same thing.

Some people condemn envious feelings. This is evident in comments like, 'And then he didn't want to come along just because he was envious.' But it is not a matter of 'just' being envious. It is an extremely painful emotion and can be a very lonely experience because the person who is envious often condemns himself for feeling that way and therefore won't talk to anyone about it.

If you sense that you have feelings of envy then what you most likely need is compassion and support to help you discover your own potential so you can start incorporating it into your life.

Talk about envy

The reason why envy manages to ruin so many relationships is because we hardly ever talk about it. The people who are experiencing the feeling are usually ashamed of it. It is simply forbidden.

If we started talking more openly about envy, a lot of problems would be solved. You could easily say, for example, 'I'm so happy for you, and at the same time it is painful for me. I wish the same thing would happen to me.'

Another example might be, 'When you talk about your new romance, I get such a feeling of longing that I can hardly breathe properly. I wish I could share in your joy. But it's hard.'

An open-hearted reply may lead to a new conversation about how the suffering party can get closer to attaining his wish or reaching his goal, since the strength of the feeling of envy depends on how much the envious person believes that he or she can reach the same goals or attain the same things. The stronger the belief that the possibility to do so exists, the less envy there will be.

Sometimes it is the envied person who must start the conversation. The envious person may feel too ashamed to want to talk about it. In such an instance, it can be helpful to hear the following comment: 'I sense that a distance emerges between us whenever I talk about my good fortune; it is as though you become less present. I just want you to know that I fully understand if it is painful for you to hear about it.'

Feelings of envy or jealousy can sometimes be so strong that you have to terminate a friendship or just take a break from it. If your friend or colleague gets the raise you yourself had hoped for it can be too painful to follow your friend's good fortune at close hand. After some months or years, you may be able to reconnect again.

Widows and widowers often decide not to socialise with happy couples during the first period after their loss because doing so tends to reopen their wounds. But after a considerable amount of time, the pain of the loss will have decreased to a level where they can contain their feelings again, even when it is intensified through the experience at close hand of seeing the love shared between couples.

But it can also be hard for those who are envied. It can get very lonely when things start to go well. The people who dream about the same things as you, and most probably also have the same kind of talent for them as you do, will sometimes find it hard to be together with you. That is sometimes the price you pay for experiencing a great success, something which I hope you would never deprive yourself of.

Avoid moralising

Some people think that envy is a bad feeling and one which we ought to be able to set ourselves above. 'It is unfair of you to be envious,' they may say. But there is no point in passing moral judgments on emotions since you cannot pick and choose them as you like. You cannot simply choose to no longer have them. And there would certainly be a price to pay if you could. That price would be repression, which often means losing a sense of vitality and purpose as well as a sense of direction in life.

However, you do have some influence over your feelings. And the best you can do to avoid burdening others with your envious feelings is to acquire the things that you want. Or let go of the hope of ever acquiring them and 'mourn' yourself through it and then set yourself some different goals that you can strive for.

If you are unable to acquire the things you long for and yet can't let go of them it may be a good idea to talk with a professional psychotherapist or coach instead of pondering over it yourself and not taking any real action.

The joy in being admired and making others envious of you

When I was a child I was for a period of time envious of my step-sister, who had received various things from her mother. The next time I visited my mother, I returned with some of my fanciest things which I had packed in a small box. I had placed tinfoil and cotton in between the various things so it took a long time to unpack it, which I did in front of my step-sister. Whether or not she got envious I don't remember, but that had certainly been my intention.

You can also hear children say with a big smile on their face after having received something new, 'Bet you don't have anything like this at home, do you?'

There can be many different motives for wanting to make others envious. It can, for example, be a way of getting revenge. It can be a form of passive-aggressive behaviour that can be difficult to work out when adults are using it. It can also be a way of standing one's ground or placing oneself in the most desirable position. Or perhaps it is just a need one has, to gain the admiration of others.

Some people are absolutely crazy about being admired. It is often because they are confusing admiration with love, and in their childhood received too much of the former and too little of the latter.

If you find yourself getting envious in a specific relationship even if you do not usually get envious, you might consider whether the other person has a hidden, most probably unconscious, agenda that involves elaborating on his or her successes in an attempt to awaken feelings of envy in others. Sometimes the presence of envy in a relationship may say more about the person who is being envied than it does about the person experiencing the envy.

A client I once had, Per, had a brother who was always talking about his successes and always with a lot of grand gesturing. It was exasperating for Per to listen to. 'But I'm probably just envious,' he would say.

I started enquiring about what the connection between them was like whenever his brother talked about his many successes. This helped Per to open up his eyes to what was actually happening. It turned out that his brother, Jakob, showed no interest in Per's inner world. The only thing Jakob sought in Per's eyes was a positive reflection and so he was expecting to receive praise, and Per had blamed himself for finding it so difficult to live up to his brother's expectations.

But it's not pleasant for anyone to be used merely as a reflection if there isn't a good connection or if the interest for one another isn't mutual.

If you find it unpleasant to listen to someone else's story about how good things are going for them, it may not necessarily be due to your own envy. Perhaps you are just being used as a tool, a thing, and no one likes to be used like that unless there is a clear and mutual agreement that those are the terms of the relationship.

Per decided to shorten the length of time that he spent with Jakob. When he no longer blamed himself for feeling that it was a strain and no longer pressured himself to endure it for so many hours at a time, he found that he had more energy to maintain their connection. And then it became easier for him to give Jakob what he so badly needed.

Summary

If you are so ashamed over your envy that you hardly dare to sense or feel it yourself, a new way or path for you may be to invite that feeling to come out into the light. Perhaps consider talking with someone else about it and find out what it is you miss in your life and how you can acquire it. If what you are missing is inaccessible, another way for you may be to embrace the sorrow entirely and then let go of it.

If you have lost a friendship or relationship owing to envy you can give it another chance by talking openly about the feeling. That applies regardless of whether it was you who experienced the envy or whether you think the other party has chosen either not to prioritise your friendship or terminated it completely because of their feelings of envy.

Chapter 8

LISTEN TO YOUR FEELINGS OF JEALOUSY

Jealousy is a despised feeling that many people are ashamed of. And some blame themselves for even feeling it while others suppress or refuse to acknowledge it to themselves or others.

If we had a choice, I think most of us would choose not to have it. However, it is not possible to merely decide that you never want to have that feeling again. There is the possibility of working on your mutual connection with the person you are jealous of to make you feel more safe and secure. It is often in relation to our partner that we feel jealousy, but it can also be in relation to a sibling, parents, friends and so on.

Jealousy is basically a fear of being out-competed. The object of your jealous feelings does not necessarily have to be a person. Perhaps you are familiar with being jealous of the television, a job or hobby that means so much to, say, your partner, so that you end up feeling less important.

Envy and jealousy resemble one another. Both contain the basic emotions: anger, sadness and happiness. Aside from that, jealousy is also the fear of being abandoned.

Many people find it easier to deal with anger than with anxiety or fear. Perhaps you can just barely feel your fear while you are completely absorbed in your anger and your desire to fight your competitor or your partner. If you dare to embrace your fear entirely and reveal it to your partner, chances that he or she will respond positively are much greater than if you merely show your anger.

If your partner is jealous

When there are feelings in play that may be associated with shame it is always important to make sure that no one ends up feeling that they are wrong. So do what you can to ensure that you can talk about it in an atmosphere of acceptance, even though you may find it difficult or are afraid of having to limit your freedom.

Perhaps you are experiencing a dilemma. If you dare present your dilemma and allow your partner to join you in finding a solution, it will benefit your relationship. The dilemma could sound something like this: 'When I see that you are in pain every time I leave, I feel like calling off everything so that I can see your smile and feel your joy. But if I choose to drop the project I am working on, a project which gives my life meaning, I am afraid that I will end up getting too frustrated, bitter and unpleasant for you to be with.' If your partner feels that he or she is important to you and has been included in your process of making a decision, his or her jealousy will automatically decrease.

Jealousy, low self-esteem and relationships

Some people more easily get jealous than others. If you are the kind of person who gets easily jealous it may be because you tend to feel your emotions very deeply. And the lower your self-esteem is, the more jealousy you will experience. If you think of yourself as someone who is less attractive, you will feel a lot more susceptible to being outdone than if you see yourself as being something special. If you tend to get the feeling that you are about to get dumped for someone else who is 'better' than you, then you would probably benefit from working on your self-esteem.

Sometimes a client will come to me who suffers from jealousy and whose partner has sent him or her to my clinic in the hope that I can remove that irritating emotion from their psyche.

However, in my experience, jealousy says a lot more about the relationship than it does about the person suffering from it. It is usually the more sensitive of the two who will sense that there is something wrong with the relationship. Perhaps the emotional warmth that there once was between the couple has started to wear off. When jealousy then emerges as a symptom it can be helpful for the couple to talk about it as a shared problem so that they can become more aware of the fact that a relationship needs to be tended to and invested in if it is going to work.

However, in some cases it makes sense for the jealous party to go to therapy and examine and work through what is hindering him or her from having a good and healthy self-esteem.

Summary

Jealousy is first and foremost a fear of being out-competed. It may be due to low self-esteem in the person experiencing it. Or it may be a sign that your relationship needs to be tended to and invested in. If you can talk about jealousy without any of you getting a sense of being wrong, then you are already well on your way to finding a solution.

Chapter 9

KNOW YOUR ANXIETY

Fear in itself is natural. Some have too little fear. They may be too rash and that can be dangerous. When we send our kids out into the world I think that most of us hope that they have enough fear ingrained in them to keep away from, for example, dangerous streets in foreign cities at night. You can have fear on various levels, ranging from a slight sense of unease to a galloping sense of panic anxiety. Some of my clients start out by telling me that they are not familiar with anxiety. But when I start explaining a little bit more about what anxiety actually is, it is often an eye-opener for them that some of the symptoms they have are, in fact, a form of anxiety. The following diagram shows a schematic presentation of various anxiety symptoms.

The people who claim never to be afraid of anything have not understood reality correctly. Life is dangerous. We will die from it and we don't know when. We don't know what tomorrow will bring, and the consequences of the choices we make today may not become apparent to us until many years later. Being a little uncertain about life is only natural.

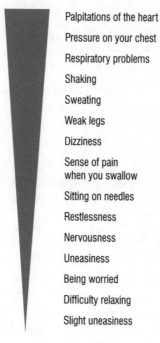

Palpitations of the heart

Pressure on your chest

Respiratory problems

Shaking

Sweating

Weak legs

Dizziness

Sense of pain
when you swallow

Sitting on needles

Restlessness

Nervousness

Uneasiness

Being worried

Difficulty relaxing

Slight uneasiness

The symptoms of anxiety

Anxiety may be a signal indicating that something is dangerous and that it would be a good idea to get away from it. But it may just as well be a sign that something means a lot to you and then it is better to move toward as opposed to away from it.

If we were to say that 0 represents no anxiety and 10 represents the maximum you can feel, then I was around an 8 the first time I was going to hold a lecture. The symptoms began the day before with a feeling of queasiness and a slight fever. Ten minutes before I was to begin my speech, my heart was pounding, and I was sweating and had trouble breathing.

I could have chosen to terminate my career as a lecturer right then and there. But my desire to share what was on my mind was so strong and meant so much to me that I chose, instead, to continue to live with the anxiety.

It is now nine years since I held my first lecture. Sometimes I can still feel the symptoms of anxiety emerge. But the pleasure I get out of doing what I am passionate about definitely outweighs the unpleasantness associated with the anxiety.

If you feel that you are unable to resist your anxiety, and sense that it hinders you from expressing yourself to the fullest, it might be a good idea to get treatment. In cognitive therapy it is possible to cure the worst of the anxiety after just a few sessions and you can learn various techniques for how you can deal with it.

However, bear in mind that it is only in rare instances that cognitive therapy can actually solve the entire problem. But, as I mentioned before, it can help you deal with the worst of it and that is definitely worth considering. It can help you to release pent-up energy so that you can work with yourself in other areas.

Anxiety is in itself not dangerous. You won't die from it. Anxiety can initiate certain processes in your body when, for example, you need to be prepared in a fight-or-flight situation, just like it does if you sense danger is near. If you thoroughly examine what anxiety actually is, and start to feel more comfortable regarding certain sensations in your body, your problem will already have started to diminish.

Summary

To feel anxiety is a natural thing. Think of it as a signal indicating that something is dangerous and telling you to hurry up and get away. Or you can interpret it as a sign that you are approaching something very important, in which case it is better to embrace the anxiety and move toward the thing that is important rather than fleeing from it.

The better you are acquainted with anxiety and its accompanying sensations in your body, the more comfortable you will feel about it. The best thing is to become good friends with your anxiety. Welcome it and allow it to be present, but never let it determine what you will or will not do.

Chapter 10

Holding Back when Feelings Grow Strong

It is seldom a good idea to take any kind of action when a feeling is at its strongest. Strong feelings tend to give us a tunnel vision that prevents us from seeing anything other than what initiated them in the first place. The larger perspectives on life tend to disappear and the short-term goals suddenly seem a lot more important than do the long-term ones.

If, for example, you are very agitated because you have received an unexpected bill, you may forget your resolution to stop smoking and grab a cigarette as a way to console yourself at that very moment. Or you may forget your long-term goal of not worrying your old mother and call her, burdening her with your frustration over the bill. Afterward you will be left with not only your feeling of disappointment over the bill but also your guilty conscience over having disregarded your own resolution.

Sometimes the art of dealing with the present moment is to not take action if you are in an angry state and most likely have momentarily lost your senses – this will only worsen the situation. Holding back instead of doing something rash when you are in a strong emotional state is something you can practise doing. You can train your skills in holding back just as you would any other skill.

When your feelings are so strong that you barely have the emotional capacity to deal with them and therefore are tempted to act upon them before thinking the situation properly through, it is a matter of having different strategies at hand that can help you delay your reaction.

Strategies for delaying impulsive actions

~ Take a warm bath or foot bath.

~ Count to ten.

~ Go for a run.

~ Call a friend.

~ Say a prayer.

~ Put on your favourite music and, possibly, sing or dance to it.

~ Embrace yourself and say something loving, as for example, 'This situation is really hard for me but I have been through similar situations before. It is not life threatening. Next summer, when I am walking on the beach, all of this will be forgotten.'

~ Make a plus–minus list. Divide a piece of paper in two and write down the advantages of your intended action on one side and the disadvantages on the other. Put the piece of paper aside and do something entirely different for a while. Then go back and read what you have written.

~ Distract yourself, by watching a movie, for example.

Think of some new methods, write them down and put the list somewhere where it is easy to find. The moment your feelings start going berserk you probably won't know what to do with yourself, in which case it is nice to have such a list with various proposals close at hand.

Once the emotional storm you have experienced has calmed down, it is time to do some self-reflection. What were those strong emotions trying to tell you? What are they saying about the situation or about your values? Is there something in your life that needs to be changed?

Summary

When you have lost your temper it is usually not a good idea to act. It is much better to put your skills in holding back to use. Perhaps you already have some good strategies that work for you. Or a new way for you could be to select some strategies either from my list or create some yourself and start practising them. The better you become at holding back, the less time and energy you will spend feeling guilty or having to smooth over the consequences of your impulsive actions. The time you save here you can invest in your long-term goals.

Chapter 11

Let Joy and Happiness Unfold

I would like to start this chapter by saying something about the kind of happiness that is real. There is a certain prestige nowadays in being happy. If you look at a dating site, most of the profiles mention something about how happy they are. An elderly lady at an old people's home once said to me, 'I am always happy... because I have to be, otherwise no one will ever want to visit me.'

When you meet a person who smiles at you, you cannot be certain that she is truly happy deep inside. A smile can be used for many things. It may signal that the person is kindly disposed toward you or it may be merely superficial, the implicit statement being, 'Look at how great I'm doing,' or 'See what a wonderful person I am.' Or maybe it's just a mask she is using to cover her anxiety or anger. If it is not pleasant to be in the presence of another person's happiness, it may be because it is not real.

It can be uncomfortable to witness a happiness that is meant more for show. It is entirely different when it comes to happiness that comes from deep inside.

Whereas anger typically gets people to shut down and concentrate on themselves, real happiness makes us soft and open. An example of the latter may be seen clearly in the film *Babette's Feast*, written by Karen Blixen and directed by Gabriel Axel.

Babette invites a frugal Norwegian congregation to dinner. The guests come from an environment that is poor not only in money but also in energy and joy. Babette has been preparing the dinner for a long period of time and the products have cost no less than a fortune. The result is an exquisite meal and we see how the mood among the guests changes and turns warm and happy. The abundance of pleasure that they experience during the dinner provides them with extra energy that allows them to give more of themselves. Old hostilities are reconciled. Love and understanding spread. In the end, everyone takes each other by the hand and dances.

Let this be an example of how investing in pleasure makes people open up more and initiates positive vibrations that may spread like ripples in water after a stone has been thrown in it.

One of the ways to experience more happiness is by being considerably thorough when planning your day so that there is room for pleasure and pleasurable activities. And with that same thoroughness be sure to encourage your loved ones to do the same and give them the space they need for it. Because joy is contagious.

A lack of joy usually becomes apparent through fatigue, and that is why you will typically want to go to bed and sleep. But rest and sleep don't help this form of tiredness, which is really a sign that your 'joy' barometer is low. In such instances, what you really have a much greater need for is joyful experiences rather than sleep.

You can examine how you stand with regard to having joy in your life by using the table below, which you also can find in Appendix 2. You can do a happiness analysis within a given week. Measure your happiness on a scale from 0 to 10. In the given week you should focus on happiness. Every time you discover that it is growing, write a number in the table. Next to the number, write a few key words about what you were doing at that very moment. For example: 4, newly mowed lawn; 7, daughter called, was feeling good; 3, the sun came out. You can see an example of a completed table in Appendix 2. (You can also find and print the table at my website.*)

Table for happiness analysis

	Monday	Tuesday	Wednesday	Thursday	Friday	Saturday	Sunday
Early morning							
Late morning							
Noon							
Afternoon							
Evening/night							

---

* https://www.highlysensitive-hsp.com/books-about-psychology/the-emotional-compass

When the week is over, you can, based on the table, determine whether there is a sufficient amount of happiness in your everyday life, or whether there is reason to put in some extra effort to increase your happiness.

If you need more joy you may find the following suggestions inspiring:

~ Buy a bouquet of flowers for yourself.

~ Take a walk out in nature and look at something beautiful.

~ Watch a good movie.

~ Enjoy a piece of art.

~ Make a nice meal, light a candle and put on your favourite music while enjoying the meal.

I suggest that you make your own list of activities that give you joy and hang them up somewhere where they are visible. You will most probably not be able to remember what they are once you are truly stressed out and need them the most.

You can find inspirational ideas for the list by looking at your weekly schedule. Concentrate on the places where joy is the greatest. Ask yourself, 'What was I doing just then that made me happy?' and 'Is it possible for me to do more of it?'

A good deed

Another way to access positive feelings is to get some work done that leaves you feeling satisfied with yourself. There is a difference between the kinds of positive feeling we are left with in terms of our actions. Take, for example, the pleasurable experience of drinking a warm cup of coffee with chocolate compared with the feeling you get after having done a job well. Both give positive feelings but in the former instance those feelings are comparatively short-lived and quickly forgotten whereas the ones in the latter example will last longer, particularly if other people have gained some joy out of what you have accomplished. Perhaps a year later you can still remember how happy your neighbour was when you shovelled snow out of his driveway, and thinking about it fills you with positive feelings of joy – and it still may do so ten years later.

When as a priest I taught candidates for Confirmation I gave them the task of going home and doing something that would make someone else feel happy and which would also bring them satisfaction. When they returned for the next class and shared what they had done, the room was filled with the kind of joy that is contagious. One had played soccer with his little brother; another had, to the great astonishment of his parents, volunteered to wash the dishes. A third had mowed the lawn. As each of them said what they had done they glowed more and more with satisfaction and joy, and the mood in the room became increasingly light and warm.

Summary

If you want to have more positive feelings in your everyday life, there are, among other things, the possibility of adding more pleasure to your life, or doing something that gives you and others joy in the long run.

Are you in the habit of allowing one day to follow the other without considering so much whether you are enjoying them? A new way for you may be to carefully plan and find time in your calendar to do something you feel like doing or that makes you feel satisfied with yourself because it is a good deed that also brings joy to others.

A third way for you to increase your sense of joy is to work on your relationships. A person's sense of well-being is to a great extent dependent on the quality of their friendships and relationships.

Chapter 12

INVEST IN YOUR RELATIONSHIPS

The better you are able to get along with the people with whom you associate, the more you will be able to thrive in your everyday life. Sometimes clients will come to me wanting to examine the extent to which a relationship can be improved. It may be with a sister, a mother, a child or a partner. For example, they might ask whether it would be an advantage to be more honest. Or would that jeopardise the relationship?

Just being able to talk about a relationship with a third person or a professional may clarify for you what it is you can contribute to the relationship.

If you experience frustration or boredom

Some people are fine with not thinking too much about what their communication is like. They enjoy being spontaneous and being able to say whatever pops up in your mind without giving it too much thought. If you are this kind of person and that method works best for you then there is no reason for you to examine the various communication models in depth.

If, on the other hand, you are looking for more depth and you tend to find spontaneous communication boring, you may enjoy familiarising yourself with the various ways in which you can become stronger and take certain steps to make a change in your communication with others.

In my book *Highly Sensitive People in an Insensitive World* (Sand 2016) I have described how you can move up or down through four different degrees of depth in a conversation and how you can practise giving and receiving more careful responses to the signals people tend to send out in their communication with one another. Since there isn't enough space in this book to give a full description of the various models, I will make do with referring to *Highly Sensitive People*.

When there is a sense of hostility or a distance between the two of you

If there is a distance between the two of you, or even downright antagonism, there are two ways you can deal with it. You can either focus on the problem or you can try to awaken a sense of joy in the other person. If you choose the former, you will most likely try to talk it over with them. At best, both you and the other person will get a chance to express what it is that is distressing or irritating you in the relationship and perhaps you will both be willing to compromise a little bit by equally taking responsibility for the negative aspects and regretting the things you have contributed that were inappropriate or not constructive for the relationship.

But it is not always possible to talk about a problem with one another. If you start out by explaining what it is you are sad or upset about, you risk the other person shutting down completely. And not everyone is ready to take their share of the blame for a problem. Some people are not strong enough to take on any responsibility for anything, in which case talking about the negative aspects will not have a liberating effect.

Another possibility is to initiate positive feelings in the relationship. If you are angry with your partner, doing something that would awaken his sense of joy may not come naturally to you. But try anyway. Give him a kiss and smile to him and say what it is you like about him, and then see what happens. Perhaps his reaction will awaken so much joy in you that whatever it was you were angry about will lose its significance and may not even have to be mentioned in the future, or if it does, perhaps it can be done in a humorous way.

When it comes to couples, I have noticed that it is typically the woman who wants to talk things over while the man would rather buy a bouquet of flowers and say something nice. The best thing is if you can switch between these two strategies. And then there are some relationships where talking the problems over just doesn't work. Read more about this in the next chapter.

Examine the relationship with a farewell letter

Whenever a client wants to work with a relationship I usually start out by giving them a letter-writing assignment: write a farewell letter to the person in question. The letter should not be given to the person; you are writing solely for your own sake. In the act of saying good-bye to someone, we are more clearly able to sense how important a role the other person played for us and in the process we become more aware of our own feelings in connection with that person.

The reason why it should be a farewell letter, as opposed to an ordinary letter, is that when we say good-bye we tend to see things in a clearer light, just as a person who is facing death does when he or she reflects on their life and discovers connections that were not apparent at the time that they were experiencing them.

You will most probably experience yourself stepping back and looking at the person from a distance as you are writing the letter. This distance makes it possible for you to see him or her not through the usual filter (consisting of your own wishes and needs) but rather for who they are as an individual. This form of distance is often an eye-opener and can give you a greater perception as to what the nature of your relationship is and what you can do to improve it.

After that you may feel like giving the letter to the person for whom it was intended. But in most cases it is better to write another letter for that purpose. This is because there happens to be a big difference between writing a letter straight from your heart in order to gain more insight into yourself and expressing your feelings, and writing a letter with the intention of opening up someone else's heart. Imagine what it would be like to be the person on the receiving end. There may be something entirely different that he or she needs to hear.

Choosing between the relationship and your personal goal

You could also ask yourself what is more important: the relationship or your personal goal. Is the most important thing getting what you want right here and now or is it having a good relationship with the other person? Some people are so focused on one aspect that they forget the other.

If you seldom reach your goals because living up to the other's expectations is very important to you, you should perhaps practise going determinedly after fulfilling your wishes, even if it means risking that your friends or co-workers will become dissatisfied with you.

If, on the other hand, you tend to run into conflicts, it may be because you are so focused on reaching your goals that you tend to overlook the significance of having a strong connection to another person. If the latter is the case, you can practise being more focused on the relationship. For example, choose one of your friendships or relationships and decide that for a period of time you want first and foremost to be focused on the relationship and less so on reaching your goals or needs. You will most likely discover that this will provide a new kind of happiness for the both of you, and that the chances that you will reach your goal in the long run will actually increase.

Summary

The relationships we choose to be in are extremely important to our sense of well-being. If you are bored in one or most of your relationships, or if there is a sense of distance or antagonism in them, it can really pay off to do what you can to improve the situation.

There are two paths you can take. If you are in the habit of confronting your problems head on and trying to talk them over, a new way for you may be to do something that increases the other person's happiness. And if you are always doing what you can to please the other person but tend to pull back when it's time to talk about something difficult, you can examine whether talking things over will give more depth and purpose to your relationship. Just be aware of the fact that the latter method does not always work for all relationships because it requires that you both have self-images that are strong and flexible.

Chapter 13

SAVE THE EXPLANATIONS

Expand Your Self-Image

We all have an image or an idea within ourselves of how we are perceived by others. The big picture is formed or shaped in childhood. We discover who we are by seeing ourselves reflected in our parents' gaze and in their reactions.

If you have parents who had the energy to take an interest in who you were as a person, and formulated it into words, then you have a strong sense of who you are. And the stronger your conviction and confidence is that you are OK as a person, the more flexible you will be able to be in your connections with others and the better you will be able to respond to the playful teasing of others with a smile.

Some of us grew up with parents who were not up to the task of familiarising themselves with who we were, and therefore couldn't help us figure it out. Maybe what they reflected to us was wrong because they only saw the things in us that they needed to see. Maybe they needed for their children to be better than those of others, and reflected us in too positive a way. Or perhaps what they saw in us was their own repressed negative sides and so they reflected us too negatively.

The areas in which you were not seen, accepted or reflected correctly by your parents as a child are the areas that will become problematic for you as an adult.

Perhaps you are uncertain as to who you are. Or perhaps you have a self-image that is ambivalent so that one minute you perceive yourself as a loser and the next a hero.

Some people have a much too limited self-image. For example, if you see yourself as a person who is always strong and can handle themselves in any situation, it will be hard for you to have to ask others for help and in general to accept yourself as weak. And if you see yourself as someone who is always helpful, it will be hard for you to set boundaries, and difficult to accept yourself when you don't have the energy to help others.

If you are unsure as to who you are, whether you are OK or not or are generally even worth loving, you will be more susceptible to what other people say about you. If someone were to imply that you are, for example, egocentric you will become very agitated and feel the urge to come up with a lot of explanations in order to convince the other person that they are completely mistaken.

Giving explanations

If you know who you are and feel good about it, you will not feel the urge to do a whole lot of explaining. You will merely show who you are.

The purpose of most explanations is to ensure that the other person perceives you in the right way; that is to say, in the way that you wish to be perceived. And that others don't perceive you in a way that you find negative.

If you constantly feel the need to explain to others what you are or are not like, you may have noticed that this sometimes irritates them. Most people would like to see and experience you in their own way. However, allowing them to do so can at times be anxiety-triggering.

Some people will start explaining away without being able to control it in the least. Perhaps they have a strong fear of abandonment because, deep down, they think that everyone will leave them if they are not seen or heard in one particular way, which was perhaps the only way for them to get any positive attention from their mother or father.

In order to be fully and truly present in the moment, people must, in their encounters with one another, have the courage to look each other in the eyes and be open to and sense one another. When encountering another person, if you dare to listen and be attentive and open to learning something completely new about both yourself and the other person, a connection of very high quality may emerge.

If you are always busy telling others what you are like, your stories may get in the way of you ever having a truly invigorating and authentic meeting with anyone.

When it is not possible to just talk things over

Some people go into therapy because they have fights that tend to go around in circles, and every time they try to talk things over it ends in anger and accusations. I ask them to sit across from one another and show me what they typically do when trying to discuss things. It usually becomes apparent that both parties have very vulnerable self-images that are somehow feeling threatened.

Perhaps the whole thing started as a conflict of interest. They disagree as to where and when to set boundaries for the children. And instead of making do with determining that there is a disagreement, voicing their opinion and making a compromise, they start explaining things – which is typically when things tend to run awry.

The purpose of her explanations is to convince him that her view of the situation is the right one and that good parenting requires that things be done her way. The problem is that her explanations come across as a criticism of him. If what she is doing is called 'good parenting', then what is his way of doing things supposed to be called? And what does it say about him in general that he supports something other than what she calls 'good parenting'? If his self-image is vulnerable he will feel that he is being attacked and will most likely defend himself by giving explanations. And in his explanations she will perceive criticism. And so the argument continues in this way.

Talking about a problem is only possible if each party is capable of seeing himself or herself as an individual who has been partially wrong. As an individual who is afraid of not being loved. As an individual who has been the reason why the other person has had difficulties. At best, you 'go Dutch', that is, you share the responsibility of taking the blame for the negative things and give each other an apology. That is what is meant by a healthy reconciliation.

But not everyone can do that. If your self-image is weak, it can be much too anxiety-producing to have to face your faults.

Some people therefore choose never to take the blame for anything. They never feel guilty because they never feel that they have done anything wrong. They will deny that they have any responsibility for the negative things with statements like, 'I had to…there was nothing else I could do.' And if you imply that he actually could have acted differently he will respond with an endless stream of explanations, and perhaps also with anger, but never an apology. He cannot face his own faults.

How to go deeper in a relationship

When we dare to express negative feelings, we move deeper into the relationship. If each party is able to express the negative aspects and accept those aspects both within themselves and in terms of the other party, it can lead to a healthy form of reconciliation in which the responsibility, for both the negative and positive aspects, is shared between the two. A good emotional connection is also possible, where one party is able to confront the other party's negative feelings without having the need to explain himself or herself. In both instances the relationship will grow deeper and feel more secure to be in.

Don't expect to be able to go deeper in all relationships. Perhaps you are not even able to go deeper in your relationship with your partner. As mentioned before, it requires that both parties are able to accept seeing themselves as individuals who make mistakes and who sometimes are the cause for other people's pain. Not everyone can do it. If your partner is unable to do that, you may well end up wasting a lot of energy trying to get him to take his part of the blame for the negative things.

And unless he himself has a strong desire to actually do it, nothing will change. And it will be a waste of time trying to talk things over. Your energy will be put to much better use if instead you try initiating something positive. Say something nice to him. He really needs it. And enjoy being together with him in the ways that work for the two of you. If you can let go of the thought that he has to have a certain depth which he doesn't have and does not wish to develop, you will better be able to appreciate the qualities that he actually has. Perhaps you can get whatever it is that is lacking in your relationship through other means. Or perhaps having a certain amount of depth in a relationship is so important to you that you will have to leave him and search for it in a different relationship.

Practise making statements
instead of explaining things

If you can make do with saying what it is you are sensing, instead of explaining how it ought to be perceived, your relationships will work much better. For example, saying, 'I can feel that I am starting to sweat,' as opposed to, 'I am the type of person who finds it difficult when others criticise me and that is due to the fact that…'

There is a much better sense of connection and intimacy in saying what you are sensing, feeling and wanting, as opposed to explaining why you feel the way you do and why you want to do certain things. There is no need for you to explain, defend or justify yourself. It is what it is. Period.

You do not need the other person's understanding. I speak with many people, especially women, who spend oceans of time and numerous words trying to get their husbands to understand why they want to do certain things. And the husband is perhaps not interested in ever understanding it because it conflicts with his wishes. So she ends up explaining and re-explaining to someone who doesn't listen. He may get irritated and even angry at all her explanations, which he never asked for in the first place. You don't need others' understanding. Say what it is you want and ask the other party to respect it. That is enough. A story 'The Hope', which you will find after this chapter, has an example of this.

It is never too late

Fortunately, it is never too late to become aware of who you really are, and feel comfortable about it. The reflection that your parents should have given you as a child is still attainable for you as an adult.

Perhaps as a grown-up you have experienced someone saying something about you and you could feel that your immediate response was, 'Yes, that is exactly what I'm like.' In moments such as these you will have added a new piece to the jigsaw puzzle that is really your self-image, making it more whole.

Sometimes a client will come to me wanting a therapeutic process that will help them find themselves. In those instances I see it as my duty to listen, accept and reflect. And in the mirroring that they get from me they will want to skip over anything useless to them and find pieces that they feel fit them on a much deeper level.

Aside from mirroring them, I also help them to obtain mirroring through other channels. The more viewpoints they attain through the mirroring, the better. I may give them this assignment to do at home: 'Ask three people the following, "What is your impression of me?" and tell me what their response was next time you see me.' For most people it is a great experience hearing what others have to say about them. Sometimes what they hear is so unrecognisable to them that it is useless. Other times they will get important information which they can use to gain more confidence in themselves.

Summary

If you have a tendency to explain a lot, a new way for you may be to work with strengthening your own inner sense of who you are. You can ask your friends to help you with this, or a professional.

The greater confidence you gain in yourself, the firmer your foundation will be and the greater courage you will have in being authentically present in your connection, without always having to make explanations.

The more acceptance and flexibility your self-image contains, and the better you become at understanding yourself, the greater your ability will be at accepting others and thereby creating a good and safe atmosphere and environment.

An ancient Greek philosopher once said:

> *To be wise is to know yourself,*
> *to know who you are*
> *and to develop the innate power within*
> *that makes you unique.*

STORY

The Hope

She hoped that he would someday understand.

She struggled to make herself understandable. Spent time trying to find the exact right words and every time she found some that could be used to describe her pain anew, she would present them to him in great anticipation. In her wishful fantasy she imagined how the expression on his face would change and he would look at her gently and say, 'Now I understand why you can't endure it.'

There was usually plenty of time to visualise and practise the words. She had learned through past experience that he needed to be forewarned. That is why she started out by carefully asking him whether he had time to talk for a little while. She hardly dared look at him as she said the words. Yet she couldn't help catching a glimpse of him through the corner of her eyes. What she saw when she looked at him just about negated any desire she may previously have had of discussing it. He looked as though she had thrown a bucket of dirty water in his face. Disassociation. He had, however, always agreed that they find a moment during the week. And that was when she would have inner dialogues with herself in order to ensure that she would be as well-formulated as possible.

She hadn't yet managed to find the right words, or at least, they hadn't had the effect that she hoped they would.

· · · · · · · · · ·

She had been on the waiting list for a consultation with psychotherapist Ole Petersen for several months. She had studied his picture on his website in advance. Still, she can't help noticing that he looks different in reality. He doesn't look like an expert. In fact, he seems a little insecure, in a sense too human, and she worries whether he is really able to help her. Whether he is the right therapist for her.

'Can you help me?' she asks while looking down at the table.

Ole Petersen sits for a little while, gazing at her as though he needs to digest her story.

'What is it you want of me?' he then asks.

She looks up in surprise. 'That you can help me find the right words that are good enough, so that I can get through to him!'

Again he sits in silence for a while and before he even opens up his mouth she has deciphered the expression on his face and knows that his answer will be negative.

'But I can teach you something new,' he adds.

· · · · · · · · · ·

Confused, she staggers out to the car. It is as though her inner jigsaw puzzle has been disassembled and the shapes of some of the pieces have been altered, making it impossible to reassemble them.

She cries all the way home. Cries over her wasted life. And to think of all the energy she had spent on trying to get him to see it from her point of view. She sees herself objectively now: begging, hoping, standing all the way up on her tippy toes to get him to understand. What a waste!

Up in the summer house there is enough tranquillity for her to try to find herself again. She takes long walks by the sea. There is a strong wind which suits her well. The whistling wind and the roar of the sea allow her to scream and cry without having to worry about whether anyone can hear her. Who cares whether her hairdo gets ruined and her face weather-beaten?

Something has been shattered inside of her: the belief that the day she manages to explain herself in the most accurate way he will put aside his own needs and give her what she has never received. And what only children can get from their parents, that is, when they are little. Why hasn't she been able to admit it until now? She herself wouldn't set aside her own needs in order to fulfil someone else's, unless it was extremely necessary or she was sure to get something back in return.

Once again she is crying over her childhood. Over that which she has fought so hard for but never got enough of. She envisions herself when she was six years old, sitting across from her father, who was reading the newspaper. She would look at him with her big, hungry eyes that were clearly saying: 'Look at me, see me for who I am, hold me!'

'Aren't you going to go out and play?' her father would say when he finally did look up.

That is how she remembered her childhood. This perpetual hunger to be at the centre of someone else's attention, to be accepted and understood. And it is as though she now can feel her sorrow a tad deeper than ever before. And at the same time it is as though something is loosening its grip on her.

After a couple of days she goes home. She goes out to the garden. She stands there for a little while observing him through the glass pane. She thinks he looks smaller and a little sad. His shoulders are stooping a little forward, indicating that he has problems of his own. She opens the garden door and senses the scent of newly sprung elderflowers. The water in the garden fountain is trickling, a sound that has always had a calming effect on her.

He turns in her direction when he hears her approaching. He looks happy. She looks directly at him. 'There is something I have to say to you.'

'Yes!' he says in surprise. An expression of seriousness replaces his smile. She sees how he holds the handle of the rake firmly, making his knuckles turn white. It is as though he is trying to get support from it.

'I hate it when you turn up the volume on the radio early in the morning.'

'Yes!'

'You don't understand that and you never will, because you don't know what it's like to have sensitive nerves.'

'No!' The furrow between his brows softens slightly.

'I can't stand it any more and I won't stand it any more.' She looks him directly in the eyes and at that very moment feels whole.

'Oh.' He glances away.

'Will you respect that?' she continues.

Now he looks at her directly as though for the first time seeing who she is.

'I suppose I'll have to.'

'Yes, if you want to live with me.'

'I do, Hanne. I've missed you.'

WRITE A
FAREWELL LETTER

Let the questions below inspire you, or write something entirely different. As long as it comes from the heart.

~ What are the pleasant things that you have lost?

~ What do you want to say 'thank you' for?

~ What is unpleasant in the relationship? What is it that you wish to free yourself of?

~ What do you wish you had received from the person?

~ What did you give in the relationship? (For example, 'I think you became happy when I...' or 'I think your pain receded when I...')

~ What would you have liked to have given more of?

~ How do you wish that your relationship had been?

~ What do you wish you could have done together with the person today?

~   What have you missed in the relationship?

~   What do you wish for the person?

Example A

Dear apartment in Højbjerg,

You housed me for four years and I thank you for that. I got to know you so well and that made me feel safe. I enjoyed the financial freedom that comes with having a low rent. It was wonderful to live close to Kirsten, and I enjoyed having three different supermarkets within biking distance.

But most of all I enjoyed the fact that you were located close to Marselisborg beach and forest. I biked out into nature when I was happy, when I was sad and when I was filled with feelings of chaos. Nature gave my soul peace.

Now I miss living close to that kind of magnificent nature. I would have liked to have been able to keep that.

But there are other things that I am happy I no longer have to deal with. I could hear noises from the neighbouring apartment which would often wake me up at night. It was beginning to irritate me to such an extent that I almost couldn't take it any more. I missed being able to sit outside in privacy. There was never any possibility for that in Højbjerg, where the windows in the next block over always made me feel that I was being observed no matter where I sat.

I will conclude by saying thank you for those four years. Thank you for all the walks in nature, the spontaneous meetings with Kirsten, the ease that comes with having a low rent and for the fact that I could bicycle everywhere. It gave me the calm I needed to work with other challenges, work which I am now able to reap the benefits of. Thank you for that.

Love,

Sofie

Example B

The letter below was written 16 years after the loss. Marianne, who has written the letter, kept dreaming that her aunt had returned and would wake up in great sorrow and frustration.

Dear Inga,

Without you my life would not have been as rich. There was an originality about you, and you had spirit. You may have been a little nuts sometimes, but never boring.

Outwardly you were charming, interested in other people and good at listening. You were the kind of person everyone wanted to be with. But few got the chance to really get to know you, and almost no one knew the extent to which you were actually suffering.

I remember that you sometimes would ask me to call the doctor in the middle of the night to demand that he come and give you a shot of pure Ketogan. Back then I didn't understand why the doctors were so reluctant to do it. Finally you couldn't take it any more. You drowned in the lake early one Whitsunday morning.

Inga, I think you did it in the best way that such things can possibly be done. Thank you for not threatening to do it beforehand like your mother did. We are thankful that you did it in a good and proper way so that we wouldn't find you injured or handicapped. Thank you for calling me three times the day before to tell me that you held no grudges against me. I was irritated that you continued to call me just to say the same thing, but I now understand that it was really out of compassion for me. Because you didn't want me to suffer afterward and because you knew that you meant a lot to me and that it would mean something.

For better or worse, you mean a lot to me. In my family I was someone whom nobody wanted to be together with. For many years I was your favourite. You liked being with me. You thought I was good at all sorts of things. You were convinced that I would do something great someday. You taught me to enjoy nature and stillness. You came and helped me when I was sick. You would light the fireplace and were wonderful at making me feel safe and listening to all my stories. We could tease each other and have fun together. How I would laugh at your woollen bloomers.

You were also an invaluable support when I became a mother at a very early age.

We had a hard time once I got married. I was 23 years old, self-absorbed and without much thought for how big a loss it was for you. You started focusing on all my faults and directed all your love at my daughter, and were completely disrespectful in your eagerness to bring her up. I froze you out of my heart. We tried to share the child, but our relationship had grown very painful and very, very difficult.

It was a relief when you kicked the bucket. I had no idea what to do.

But now I miss you, Inga. Miss our relationship as it was before I got married. You would have been proud of me if you could see me now. You should have seen Eva grow up. We should have shared the joy in seeing that together. You would have been so happy to see how good things are going.

Inga, I have dreams about you at night. I dream that you are here but that you have just not wanted to see me for a while. I always wake up just before connecting with you on the telephone, my heart in my mouth, saying the words, 'Inga, won't you please see me again? I miss you so.'

I would so much like to see you, just one more time. I won't touch you so much, I know you don't like that. If I could just place my hand on your shoulder and look into your eyes and say thank you. Thank you for everything that you have given me. Thank you because you could see something big and great in me. Thank you for all the inspiration. You were really a person who dared go her own way. Much of what is going well in my life now is due to the things you taught me.

I often think about whether I could have helped you if you were still with us today.

You took the ticket. You believed in reincarnation and assumed you'd start over.

I hope with all my heart that things worked out for you the way you wanted them to. That you have started over among good and loving people. Or that you are with God in heaven. I hope he is rocking you in his arms and saying, 'You have had a hard life, Inga. Good thing that you have come home here where no sorrows can reach you.' But if you would rather be reincarnated then I hope that that is what happened. I wish you all the best.

A thousand loving greetings from

Marianne,
who will never forget you.

Afterword

When Marianne read the letter aloud we both cried. It was a strong experience. Marianne later told me that from that day on the dreams ceased coming. And where earlier it had been extremely painful for her to even think of Inga, she was now able to recall her with a sense of sorrow, peace and thankfulness.

Tables for Happiness Analysis

	Monday	Tuesday	Wednesday	Thursday	Friday	Saturday	Sunday
Early morning							
Late morning							
Noon							
Afternoon							
Evening/ night							

	Monday	Tuesday	Wednesday	Thursday	Friday	Saturday	Sunday
Early morning		Coffee on the terrace 4			Homemade rolls 3		Cosying up in bed 9
Late morning	Received recognition at work 7		Received invitation 5	Finished writing report 7		Cleaned 3	
Noon	Colleague asked for my advice 3	After taking a jog 6	Sat out in the sun 8	Received sweet text message from Jens 6	Enjoyed lunch 4		Plants blooming 3
Afternoon		Said no in a difficult situation 4	Picked up new books at the library 3	My favourite tea was on sale 3	Colleague recognised the fact that I am a listener 2	Had a long bath 4	
Evening/ night		Sister called 6	Delicious dinner 4		Candlelight and star-gazing 7	Danced 8	Confidential dialogue 6

Thanks to...

Registered psychotherapist and theologian Bent Falk, whose wise and intelligent words I have been listening to with pleasure in various contexts through the years and whose guidance has helped me to discover sides to myself that I didn't know existed.

Graduate of applied psychology and head of the Institute for Gestalt Analysis, Niels Hoffmeyer, who has been a great source of inspiration, owing to his simple and precise way of expressing himself when describing the human psyche, making his listeners sigh with relief in recognition of his words.

Graduate of applied psychology Peter Storgård, who taught me the importance of following psychological research and showed me the potential of cognitive therapy.

A thank-you to all of you whom I have spoken with as a therapist or in my practice and to those of you who have gone to my lectures or my courses. A special thanks to those of you who have given me permission to use your stories in this book.

Also thank you to those of you who have read through the manuscript of this book and provided me with feedback. Without that sparring which I have shared with you, the book would not have been nearly as precise in its articulation and expression. I would especially like to mention Martin Håstrup, Janet Cecilie Ligaard, Kirstine Sand and Pia Skadhede. You have each in your own way left your mark on this book.

BIBLIOGRAPHY

Beck, J.S. (2011) *Cognitive Behavior Therapy: Basics and Beyond* (Second Edition). New York, NY: Guilford Press.

Buber, M. (2010) *I and Thou*. Eastford, CT: Martino Fine Books.

Davidsen-Nielsen, M., and Leick, N. (1991) *Healing Pain: Attachment, Loss, and Grief Therapy*. London: Routledge.

Knudsen, P.Ø. (1998) *Passioner: Atten stafetsamtaler*. Copenhagen: Gyldendal.

Miller, A. (1997) *The Drama of the Gifted Child*. New York, NY: Basic Books.

O'Toole, D. (1988) *Aarvy Aardvark Finds Hope*. Burnsville, NC: Compassion Press.

Rosenberg, M.B. (2003) *Non-violent Communication: A Language of Life*. Encinitas, CA: Puddledancer Press.

Sand, I. (2016) *Highly Sensitive People in an Insensitive World: How to Create a Happy Life*. London: Jessica Kingsley Publishers.

Selva, D., and Coughlin, P. (1996) *Intensive Short-term Dynamic Psychotherapy: Theory and Technique*. London: Karnac Books.

Yalom, I.D. (1980) *Existential Psychotherapy*. New York, NY: Basic Books.

Young, J.E. (1990) *Cognitive Therapy for Personality Disorders: A Schema-Focused Approach*. Sarasota, FL: Professional Resource Exchange.

INDEX

Page numbers in *italics* refer to figures and tables.

Ilse Sand is a Theology graduate from the University of Aarhus, where she wrote her Master's thesis on C.G. Jung and Søren Kierkegaard. She is also trained in several psychotherapeutic approaches and is registered with the Association for Psychotherapy in Denmark. After being employed for several years as a parish priest for the Danish National Church she now works as a supervisor, trainer, speaker and therapist.

See more at www.highlysensitive-hsp.com